DAT®

Lesson Book

Course Companion

Special thanks to the team that contributed to this book:

Mike Aebly, Khal Albaba, Matt Belinkie, Kim Bowers, Josh Brooks, Matt Burke, Aaron Cate, Kay Christensen, Mike Costa, Sumir Desai, Boris Dvorkin, Tim Eich, Samantha Fallon, Tyler Fara, Elizabeth Flagge, Joanna Graham, Adi Hanash, Justine Harkness, Allison Harm, Beth Hoffberg, Ali El Husseiny, Ae-Ri Kim, Stuart Kovinsky, Liz Laub, Tami Miller, Chris Murphy, Matt Rasmussen, Larry Rudman, Teresa Rupp, Amjed Saffarini, Tom Sargent, Eli Schwartz, J. Ethan Sterling, Rebecca Stover, Stephen Sylwestrak, Chris Thipphavong, Lee Weiss, Mike Welch

Published by Kaplan Publishing, a division of Kaplan, Inc.
750 Third Avenue
New York, NY 10017

ISBN: 978-1-5062-3575-2

10 9 8 7 6 5 4 3 2

TABLE OF CONTENTS

STRATEGY 1

TOPICS COVERED

- The Kaplan DAT Course
- The DAT
- Kaplan DAT Strategies
- Your DAT Study Plan

After this session you will be able to:

- Describe the sections of the DAT and their scoring systems
- Formulate a personal study calendar that includes all the necessary actions from now until Test Day
- Recall the steps of Kaplan's question, answer choice, and CBT strategies

The Kaplan DAT Course

Goal: Earn a higher score on your DAT and get the results you want.

What will this course include?

- Content
- Strategies
- Study Planning
- Crisis Prevention

The DAT

Scoring

Score	Basis
Biology	performance on questions 1–40 of the Survey of the Natural Sciences section
General Chemistry	performance on questions 41–70 of the Survey of the Natural Sciences section
Organic Chemistry	performance on questions 71–100 of the Survey of the Natural Sciences section
Total Science	performance on all questions (1–100) in the Survey of the Natural Sciences section; not simply an average of the three subsection scores
Reading Comprehension	performance on all questions in the Reading Comprehension section
Quantitative Reasoning	performance on all questions in the Quantitative Reasoning section
Academic Average	the simple arithmetic average of the following five standard scores, rounded to the nearest whole number: Biology, General Chemistry, Organic Chemistry, Reading Comprehension, and Quantitative Reasoning
Perceptual Ability	performance on all questions in the Perceptual Ability section; does not constitute any component of any other reported score

Distribution of Scores by Percentile

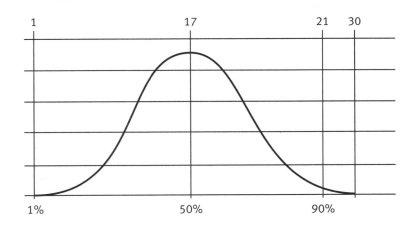

Setting Expectations

Student	Diagnostic	FL 1	FL 2	FL 3	FL 4	FL 5	Δ
A	15	16	17	17	17	17	2
B	16	17	19	19	19	19	3
C	19	18	21	20	19	25	6
D	11	16	17	17	16	18	7
E	13	16	17	18	17	20	7
F	16	20	23	22	22	23	7

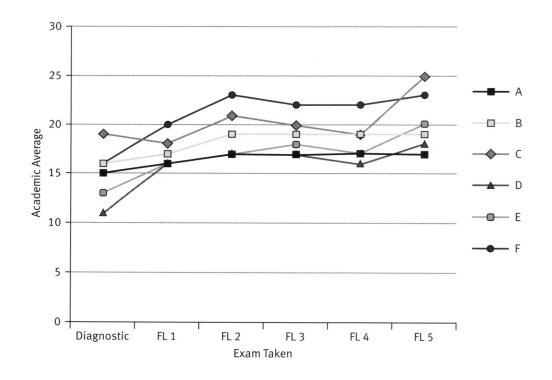

Your Goal Score

My target score is _____

The reason this is my target score is because _____

The three biggest obstacles to me achieving this score are:

1. _____

2. _____

3. _____

I can overcome these obstacles by:

1. _____

2. _____

3. _____

Test Day Outline

Section Name	Time	Questions	Topics
Survey of the Natural Sciences	90 min.	100	Biology, General Chemistry, Organic Chemistry
Perceptual Ability	60 min.	90	Keyholes, Top-Front-End, Angle Ranking, Hole Punching, Cube Counting, Pattern Folding
BREAK	30 mins.	-----	-----
Reading Comprehension	60 min.	50 (3 passages, 16–18 questions each)	Passages from medical and natural sciences
Quantitative Reasoning	45 min.	40	Algebra, Numerical Calculations, Conversions, Probability & Statistics, Geometry, Trigonometry, Word Problems

Kaplan DAT Strategies

Pacing

Triaging

Get your easy points first.

Complete Every Section

Answer every question.

Pacing by Section

Use Kaplan's Strategies for pacing yourself on each individual section of the test.

The Kaplan Question Strategy

STOP

→ Triage: Should you do this question now, later, or never?

THINK

→ What is the question really asking?

PREDICT

→ Formulate a framework or prediction for your answer.

MATCH

→ Select the answer that truly meets the requirements of the prediction.

A Worked Example

1. Fifteen movie theaters average 600 customers per day. If 6 are shut down, but the same number of people still attend the movies, what is the new average attendance for the movie theaters that remain open?

   A.   100
   B.   500
   C.   900
   D.   1,000
   E.   1,500

Expert Thinking

STOP

Answers are numbers that are far apart. This question requires rough calculation where estimation could be sufficient.

THINK

The question is asking for the new average attendance given a smaller number of open theaters but the same number of customers.

PREDICT

First, find the total number of customers. Before any closures, there were 15 theaters with 600 customers each. When multiplied, this comes to 9,000 customers. Now there are only 9 theaters open. 9,000 divided by 9 gives an average of 1,000 customers per day for each theater.

MATCH

The final answer should be 1,000 customers, which matches answer choice (D).

Kaplan Answer Choice Strategy

Wrong Answer Choice Pathologies

Pathology	Why It's Wrong	Why It's Seductive
Faulty Use of Detail		
Opposite		
Distortion		
Out of Scope		
Miscalculation		

Kaplan Computer-Based Test Strategy

Overview

Computer-Based Testing Tools

- Review Button
- Mark Button
- Highlighting
- Calculator (Quantitative Reasoning)

Test Question Interface

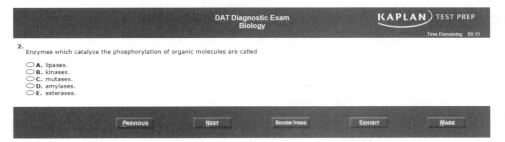

Review Page Interface

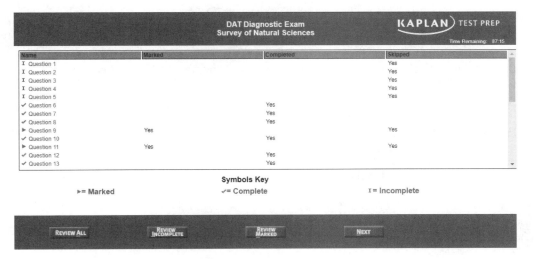

Skipping Strategy

- Non-Reading Comprehension
- Reading Comprehension

Scratch Work Strategy

- Maximizing Area for Scratch Work
- Non-writing Hand and the Mouse

Your DAT Study Plan

Using Your Kaplan Resources Effectively

Diagnostic

Your Diagnostic is critical for establishing a baseline and guiding your prep.

Preview Homework

Complete the assigned Preview Homework prior to each session.

Class Sessions

Attend all required sessions or view as Lessons On Demand. Have your Lesson Book on hand for every class and use it to take notes.

Review Homework

Complete your Review Homework within 24 hours of your lesson if at all possible.

Full-Length Exams

Use full-length practice tests to mimic Test Day.

Additional Resources

Several additional resources are available on your Online Syllabus and in your Home Study Kit to help you maximize your DAT score.

Building a Study Plan

Register for Your DAT

Create a Study Calendar

The Dirty Dozen

#12: Doing the same thing as everybody else

#11: Letting stress get in the way

#10: Timing yourself in the beginning

#9: Focusing on difficulty levels

#8: Testing under non-testlike conditions

#7: Not committing to your study schedule

#6: Listening now but studying later

#5: Only studying the right answers

#4: Ignoring your strengths

#3: Forgoing explanations and mistakes

#2: Making it about the number, not the process

#1: Taking test after test after test

READING COMPREHENSION 1

TOPICS COVERED

- The Reading Comprehension Section
- Kaplan Method for Reading Comprehension
- Reading Strategically
- The Kaplan Question Strategy
- Question Types

After this session you will be able to:

- Recall Kaplan's strategies for reading strategically and classifying Reading Comprehension question types

The Reading Comprehension Section

Overview

- 50 questions across 3 passages in 60 minutes.
  - · Each passage is 9–14 paragraphs long.
  - · Each passage has 16–18 questions.
- Familiarity with the subject matter is not required.
  - · Subject areas: natural and medical sciences.
- Every operational question within Reading Comprehension counts equally toward your score.

Pacing

- Spend approximately 20 minutes per passage.
  - · Use 7–8 minutes to read and map the passage.
  - · Save 12–13 minutes for the questions, giving yourself about 45 seconds per question.

Kaplan Method for Reading Comprehension

READ STRATEGICALLY

- ➜ Preview the passage for Topic.
- ➜ Anticipate while reading using Keywords.
- ➜ Map each paragraph's Scope.
- ➜ Determine the author's Tone.
- ➜ Identify the author's overall Purpose.

passage title or 1st sentence — thing talked about overarching Ideas.

— anticipate content / Dogs e.g.

whats the concept

Positive about dogs e.g. Feeling about topic

Whats the point (argue dogs are Best pets)

why is author giving info

Reading Strategically

Preview the Passage for Topic

Topic is the author's basic subject matter.

The passages on the test will be titled according to the Topic.

Scope

Telescopes: Refractors Versus Reflectors

topic

(1). The earliest telescopes were refractors, in that they used lenses to bend incoming light. By using refractive lenses, early astronomers were able to gather light and view images with greater resolution and magnification than possible with the naked eye. But because pioneer telescope makers knew relatively little about optics, their lenses exhibited two serious defects. The first problem, spherical aberration, is a distortion that occurs when a lens with round surfaces fails to focus light from a point object to a point image. The second problem, chromatic aberration, stems from the fact that an ordinary lens refracts different wavelengths of light to slightly different degrees, resulting in a different focal length for each color and, therefore, an out-of-focus image with a colorful halo.

(2). A number of scientists, among them Johannes Kepler, realized that spherical aberration could be corrected simply by using a differently shaped lens. A solution to chromatic aberration, however, proved more difficult. When Sir Isaac Newton announced that it seemed impossible to correct chromatic aberration, scientists turned their attention to reflecting telescopes. Like refractors, these telescopes also increased light, resolution, and magnification of an image, but reflectors use curved mirrors in lieu of clear lenses in order to avoid the chromatic distortion of refraction. However, early reflecting telescopes had their problems too: the mirrors they utilized were made of metal alloys, which absorbed light and thus obscured images. One solution to this problem was to build larger telescopes, since bigger mirrors mean greater light reception and brighter images. Unfortunately, the opticians and foundries of the day were not yet up to the challenge. Mirror technology progressed slowly, as did the development of better reflector telescopes.

(3). Chromatic aberration remained a problem in refractors until Englishman Peter Hall discovered that a compound lens (i.e., one that combined different surfaces) could compensate for the dispersion of different colors by focusing them back together. Unfortunately, his findings were little known. Later, mathematician Leonhard Euler hit upon a similar solution using two lenses with water between them. Soon after, noted optician John Dollond followed Euler's lead and sandwiched a piece of flint glass between two pieces of crown glass, an arrangement that corrected both chromatic and spherical aberration. As a result of this advancement and subsequent modifications, the refractor once again became the telescopic instrument of choice and remained so for about 100 years.

(4). But the refractor continued to have one inescapable limitation—a constraint on the maximum effective lens diameter, which limits the light-gathering property of the telescope. For this reason, as well as because of technical advances in mirror making, the reflector would once again assume prominence. At the Great Exposition of 1851, Varnish and Mellish presented the first chemical technique for layering silver onto glass. The mirrors that ultimately resulted from this breakthrough were silvered on the front and represented a double advantage. First, the silver surface (financially feasible because of the small amount of silver required) increased reflectivity of mirrors some 50 percent. Second, using glass in place of metal eliminated problems of shrinkage and cracking.

(5). The refractor never again surpassed the reflector. With further advances in the development of heat-resistant glass and casting techniques, larger and larger mirrors became possible, and astronomers saw farther and farther into the universe.

Anticipate While Reading Using Keywords

Keywords are structural clues that every author uses to organize and shape the text.

The best critical readers pick up on these structural clues and are thus able to anticipate while reading.

Keywords in Context

Astronomers noted more than 150 years ago that sunspots wax and wane in number in an 11-year cycle. Ever since, people have speculated that the solar cycle might exert some influence on the earth's weather. In the 20th century, for example, workers linked the solar cycle to droughts in the American Midwest. Until recently, however, none of these correlations has held up under closer scrutiny.

An example follows

don't need to Read

Types of Keywords

1. Continuation

(handwritten: can skip or go faster)

Continuation keywords indicate that more of the same idea or argument will follow. A subtype of Continuation keywords is Illustration keywords, which introduce examples the author uses to elaborate on a point.

Examples: *also, in addition, for example, moreover, furthermore, as well as, for instance, and such as*

2. Sequence

(handwritten: skip or move fast)

Sequence keywords denote an order of ideas, points, or events.

Examples: *second, first*

3. Evidence

(handwritten: slow down take notice)

Evidence keywords are clues that the author is about to provide support for a point.

Examples: *because, since for, the reason that*

4. Contrast

Stop and Pay attention

Contrast keywords indicate that something different is coming next or that the author is making a shift in focus.

Examples: But, nevertheless, alternatively however, despite, initially, although

5. Emphasis

Slow down *author opinion!*

Emphasis keywords highlight the elements of the passage that the author finds most important.

Examples: above all, essentially, clearly most of all, especially

6. Conclusion

Stop and read

Conclusion keywords signal the sum of an argument.

Examples: thus, in conclusion Consequently, So, it follows that,

---

TAKEAWAY

Identifying Keywords on Test Day can help you to not only anticipate what will come next in the passage, but also to anticipate what the DAT will ask about in the questions.

Map Each Paragraph's Scope

Scope is the specific aspect of the Topic on which the author focuses.

e.g., chromatic aberration problems

Practice

BPI

Genetic engineering may offer the best hope of improving yields of ~~Oryza sativa~~ (cultivated rice) and perhaps, in time, other important US crops. The insertion of foreign genetic material into the DNA of cultivars appears to confer an herbicidal protection on the resultant plants, enabling them to compete successfully for nutrients with uncultivated grasses.

Topic: *Genetic engineering*

Scope: *Results improvements in Rice*

Media coverage of Alzheimer's disease, an ultimately fatal form of dementia that primarily afflicts the elderly, generally focuses on the disease itself: the difficulty of establishing a diagnosis and the lack of any effective treatment. Far less attention is paid to the tremendous physical, psychological, and financial toll that the disease takes on family members who live with and care for Alzheimer's patients 24 hours a day.

Topic: *Alzheimer's*

Scope: *Media Attention to caregivers*

Creating a Roadmap

The key to success on the Reading Comprehension section is structured, targeted mapping.

The Roadmap is a diagram of the passage noting the Scope of each paragraph. A good Roadmap helps you find information in the passage quickly.

Sample Roadmap

P1   Q1–16

¶1   *1st telescopes = refractors; 2 probs*

¶2   *try reflectors; also probs*

¶3   *fix refractor chromatic aberration prob*

¶4   *refractor still limited*
       mirrors ↑ reflectors

¶5   *reflector › refractor*

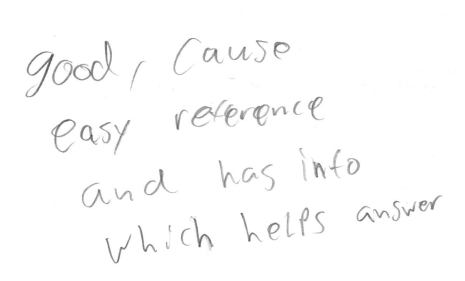

1: Navigating
2: maintaining focus
3: contains answers

good, cause
easy reference
and has info
which helps answer

Using Your Roadmap

1. Of the following, the author is most interested in discussing

   A. how different shapes of lenses influence resolution and magnification in telescopes.

   B. why refractors have become more popular than reflectors.

   C. how two basic telescope designs alternately succeeded each other in importance and popularity.

   D. the ways in which technological constraints have shaped the course of science.

   E. the ways dispersion impacts the resolution in telescopes.

2. The author mentions the views of Sir Isaac Newton (paragraph 2) in order to

   A. explain why scientists initially turned toward reflecting telescopes.

   B. emphasize the severity of the problem of spherical aberration.

   C. show that early scientists often reached erroneous conclusions.

   D. tacitly challenge the view that Sir Isaac Newton was a brilliant scientist.

   E. give the history of the first refractor telescopes used.

3. According to the passage, chromatic aberration can be corrected by

   A. a lens with rounded surfaces.

   B. using glass in place of metal alloys.

   C. building larger telescopes for greater light reception.

   D. an arrangement of two lenses separated by water.

   E. rotating the lenses between 15° and 30°.

Identify the Author's Overall Purpose

Purpose is the reason why the author is writing the passage. Identifying the Purpose will help you to understand the passage as a whole. All of the details in the passage are meant to support the author's overall Purpose.

The Purpose should always be given in verb form.

> *Explain, Evaluate, Argue, Compare*

Before moving on to the questions, you should create a Purpose sentence in your mind to solidify your understanding of the passage. If the author's attitude towards the subject is not neutral, this should also be noted within your Purpose.

Crisis Prevention

What if I don't know what to map?

What if I am running out of time?

What if I don't know the meaning of a word?

TAKEAWAY

Reading strategically can help you not only to anticipate what will come next in a passage but also to anticipate what the DAT will ask about in the questions.

Passage 1

The Harbor Seal

(1). The harbor seal, *Phoca vitulina*, is a member of the order Pinnipedia and lives amphibiously along the northern Atlantic and Pacific coasts. This extraordinary mammal, which does most of its fishing at night when visibility is low and where noise levels are high, has developed several unique adaptations that have sharpened its visual and acoustic acuity. The need for such adaptations has been compounded by the varying behavior of sound and light in each of the two habitats of the harbor seal—land and water.

(2). While the seal is on land, its ear operates much like that of a human, with sound waves traveling through air and entering the inner ear through the auditory canal. The directions from which sounds originate are distinguishable because the sound waves arrive at each inner ear at different times. In water, however, where sound waves travel faster than they do in air, the ability of the brain to differentiate arrival times between each ear is severely reduced. Yet it is crucial for the seal to be able to pinpoint the exact origins of sound in order to locate both its offspring and prey. Therefore, through processes of adaptation to the demands of its environment, the seal has developed an extremely sensitive quadraphonic hearing system, composed of a specialized band of tissue that extends down from the outer ear to the inner ear. In water, sound is conducted to the seal's inner ear by this special band of tissue, making it possible for the seal to identify the exact origins of sounds.

Scratch Work

Paragraph 1

P1) Harbor Seal adaptations (+)

Paragraph 2

P2) Seal hearing adaptations

(3). The eye of the seal is also uniquely adapted to operate in both air and water. The human eye, adapted to function primarily in air, is equipped with a cornea, which aids in the refraction and focusing of light onto the retina. As a result, when a human eye is submerged in water, light rays are further refracted and the image is blurry. The seal's cornea, however, has a refractive index similar to that of water. Therefore, in water, light rays are transmitted by the cornea without distortion and are clearly focused on the retina. In air, however, the cornea is astigmatic. The result is a distortion of incoming light rays. The seal compensates for this by having a stenopaic pupil, which constricts into a vertical slit. Since the astigmatism is most pronounced in the horizontal plane of the eye, the vertical nature of the pupil serves to minimize its effect on the seal's vision.

(4). Since the harbor seal procures its food under conditions of low visibility, some scientists hypothesize that harbor seals have an echolocation system akin to the sensory capabilities of bats, porpoises, and dolphins. This kind of natural and instinctual radar involves the emission of high frequency sound pulses that reflect off of obstacles such as predators, prey, or natural barriers. The reflections are received as sensory signals by the brain, which interprets them and processes them into an image. The animal, blinded by unfavorable surroundings or lighting conditions, is thus able to perceive its surroundings. Scientists believe that echolocation in the harbor seal is suggested by the fact that these seals emit "clicks," i.e., high-frequency sounds produced in short, fast bursts that occur mostly at night, when visual acuity is low.

Scratch Work

Paragraph 3

P 3) Seal Vision, Water Vs Land

Paragraph 4

P 4) Seals may have echolocation

(5). Finally, there is speculation that the seal's vibrissae, or whiskers, act as sensory receptors. Evidence for this is found in the fact that vibrissae are unusually well developed in Pinnipedia and are highly sensitive to movement. Scientists hypothesize that the vibrissae may be instrumental in catching prey and, because they are sensitive to vibrations, may sense wave disturbances produced by nearby moving fish, allowing the seal to home in on and capture prey.

(6). Having met the sensory demands of dual habitats, the harbor seal is one of the most interesting animals on earth. Its amphibious existence has demanded a sensory acuity and flexibility matched by few other mammals.

Scratch Work

Paragraph 5

Whiskers

Paragraph 6

Seals are Interesting

Purpose

They think Seals
are Interesting
and here is why

explain harbor
seal adaptations
and (+)

The Kaplan Question Strategy

STOP

→ Characterize the question type.

THINK

→ What is the question really asking?

→ Where is the relevant information you need?

PREDICT

→ Formulate a framework or prediction for your answer.

MATCH

→ Select the answer that truly meets the requirements of the prediction.

Question Types

There are six main question types in the Reading Comprehension section of the DAT.

If you understand how to approach each question type, you can more easily attack questions on Test Day.

Global Questions

Global questions ask for the general purpose or main idea of the passage. Predict the answer using your Purpose sentence.

Examples of question stems:

- *The main purpose of the passage is to . . .*
- *Which one of the following best states the main idea of the passage?*
- *Which one of the following best describes the organization of the passage?*
- *The passage can best be described as . . .*

Practice

4. The main purpose of the passage is to

    A.   discuss how the harbor seal fishes at night.
    B.   explain the adaptations of the harbor seal in its two habitats.
    C.   evaluate the effectiveness of the harbor seal's hearing on land.
    D.   compare the way a harbor seal uses echolocation on land and in water.
    E.   argue that the harbor seal is the mammal with the best night vision.

Detail Questions

Detail questions are the most common question type on the DAT. The answer to a Detail question can be found directly in the passage. Refer back to the passage to see what was stated in order to formulate your prediction. Variations on the Detail question type are common. One common variation on the Detail question type is a question stem that presents you with one to two statements with answer choices that require you to determine whether or not the question stem material is from the passage.

Examples of question stems:

- *According to the passage ...*
- *As stated in the passage ...*
- *[Statement 1.]*
  [Statement 2.]

Practice

5. According to the passage, the sensitivity of the harbor seal's whiskers to vibrations is most beneficial for

   A. triggering fish in surrounding areas to move about.
   B. improving the seal's ability to smell nearby predators.
   C. enhancing the seal's balance on land.
   D. perceiving wave disturbances produced by prey.
   E. sensing echolocation waves produced by other seals.

Detail EXCEPT Questions

These questions are similar to Detail questions, but they will use words like *EXCEPT* or *NOT*. More research in the passage will be required to get these questions right. The questions are not necessarily difficult, but can be more time-consuming.

Examples of question stems:

- *Each of the following statements is used as evidence in the passage EXCEPT one. Which one is the EXCEPTION?*
- *According to the passage, which of the following is NOT true …*

Practice

6. According to the passage, all of the following are true about the harbor seal's quadraphonic hearing system EXCEPT one. Which is the EXCEPTION?

   A.   It is composed of a specialized band of tissue.
   B.   It extends from the outer ear to the inner ear.
   C.   It is used to conduct sound in water to the seal's inner ear.
   D.   It is used mostly on land, where sound waves travel more slowly.
   E.   It helps the seal to pinpoint the exact origins of sounds originating from its offspring.

Function Questions

Function questions will ask you why or how the author used certain tools to build their argument. These questions may ask you about the purpose of individual paragraphs or about the relationships between evidence and conclusions that were stated in the passage. Use your Roadmap and refer back to the passage to find the answer.

Examples of question stems:

- *The author of the passage refers to X in order to ...*
- *In the second paragraph, the author of the passage is primarily concerned with ...*
- *[Statement + Reasoning]*

Practice

7. The author mentions other mammals such as bats, porpoises, and dolphins in paragraph 4 in order to

   A. provide examples of other animals that use echolocation.
   B. substantiate the claim that seals use a stenopaic pupil.
   C. explain a type of instinctual radar used by seals.
   D. contrast the harbor seal's "clicks" with the high-frequency sounds of other animals.
   E. support the scientific hypothesis that adaptations are most important at night.

8. Seals have a highly sensitive hearing system because they have adapted to be able to hear both ~~predators~~ *Prey* and their own offspring.

   A. Both the statement and the reason are correct and related.
   B. Both the statement and the reason are correct but NOT related.
   C. The statement is correct, but the reason is NOT.
   D. The statement is NOT correct, but the reason is correct.
   E. NEITHER the statement NOR the reason is correct.

Inference Questions

To answer an Inference question correctly, you must make a small logical leap from the passage. Be careful—the correct answer will be extremely similar to what you actually read. Only the answer that must be true based on the passage is correct.

Examples of question stems:

- *It can be inferred from the passage that the author would be most likely to agree with which one of the following?*
- *The passage suggests which one of the following about ... ?*
- *Based on the passage ...*
- *The passage implies that ...*

Practice

9. Based on the passage, it can be inferred that

    A. humans also have a stenopaic pupil.
    B. bats, porpoises, and dolphins have an astigmatic cornea.
    C. the refractive index of a seal's cornea differs from that of a human's.
    D. light rays are distorted when a seal is in water.
    E. the seal's retina is more effective than a human's retina.

eyes

P3

Other Questions

The Other question type encompass a few relatively unique questions types that occur **very** infrequently on the DAT. The first type of question to fall into the Other category are referred to as Strengthen/Weaken questions, which ask you to interpret new information and determine what effect the new information has on the passage. With Strengthen/Weaken questions, you should consider the argument made in the passage and how the new information either makes it more likely (strengthen) or less likely (weaken) to be true. The second Other question type can be referred to as Tone questions, which test how the author feels about something in the passage. Tone questions are most easily addressed by ensuring you are tracking the author's attitude (positive, negative, neutral) while reading and making your Roadmap.

Examples of question stems:

- *Which phrase from paragraph 5 reflects a negative bias?*
- *Which of the following statements, if true, would most strengthen the theory put forth in paragraph 3?*

Practice

10. Suppose that the walrus, *Odobenus rosmarus*, also from the order Pinnipedia, is found to use its vibrissae to sense differences in shapes while grazing along the seafloor, thereby enabling it to detect mollusks and other organisms that comprise the walrus's diet. How would this new information impact the author's argument about the harbor seal?

   A. This would provide evidence against the author's claims about the way the harbor seals use their vibrissae for sensory receptors in water.

   B. This would support the author's theory that the walrus developed before the harbor seal.

   C. This would conflict with the author's claim that the vibrissae in harbor seals are unusually well developed.

   D. This would offer a supporting illustration of how other pinnipeds use vibrissae to home in on prey.

   E. This would present a case substantiating the author's hypothesis that pinnipeds are the only animals to use their whiskers as sensory receptors.

> **TAKEAWAY**
> Determining what type of question is being asked helps you to think only about the most relevant material and to make an informed prediction.

Passage 2

Dental Caries

(1). The development of dental caries is characterized by bacteria-induced destruction of the mineral and organic components of the tooth's enamel and underlying dentin. It is a progressive process. The initial lesion can, if untreated, expand to involve the tooth's pulp, which consists of connective tissue supplied with nerve fibers and blood vessels. Pulpal involvement can lead to inflammation and a variety of symptoms, including pain after the consumption of sugar and a throbbing sensation associated with thermal hypersensitivity. If still untreated, the oral infection eventually can affect systemic health. The initiation of dental caries is highly dependent on the microenvironment of the host's oral cavity and involves complex interactions between the host, bacteria and their metabolic products, and the calcified tissues of the teeth.

(2). In the 19th century, Louis Pasteur showed that certain microorganisms convert sugars to lactic acid and that a resulting acidic environment can cause the dissolution of tooth surfaces. In experiments conducted with three groups of young rats in the 1950s, researchers fed one group a cariogenic diet under germ-free conditions; no caries developed. A second group, which included the first group's littermates, was also fed a cariogenic diet but was infected with a specific bacterial strain; caries developed. A control group was raised in a normal environment and fed a cariogenic diet; caries also developed in this group.

(3). Experts generally now agree that dental caries is caused by specific bacteria indigenous to the human oral cavity, such as *Streptococcus mutans*. The preliminary event in the development of caries is deposition on the tooth's surface of plaque, a complex aggregation of salivary proteins, bacteria, dietary nutrients, and minerals. Such deposition is initiated by a thin film of salivary proteins that coats a tooth's surface. The proteins attach to the tooth by ionic interactions between their polar sulfate and ammonium groups and the calcium ions contained in the organic matrix of the tooth's enamel. In turn, the sticky dextrans that are part of the bacteria's extracellular coats enable the microorganisms to attach to the salivary proteins.

(4). The bacteria, which thrive in acidic conditions, convert carbohydrates to organic acids, such as lactic acid, and produce proteolytic enzymes. The organic acids lower the pH at the plaque-enamel interface, and calcium salts in the enamel are slowly dissolved due to the acidic conditions. Once the salts in the tooth's enamel have dissolved, proteolytic enzymes can attack and digest the organic matrix of the enamel. Nevertheless, enamel is the primary barrier to the development of dental caries and is far more resistant to demineralization than is the underlying dentin.

(5). The replication and degree of metabolic activity of oral bacteria are strongly dependent on the availability of carbohydrates. The diets of many people in industrialized nations—high in sucrose and other sugars—supply the bacteria with a preferential metabolic substrate, strongly activating their metabolic systems and facilitating the carious process. Other host factors that affect the incidence of dental caries are salivary composition and flow rate, the physiochemical nature of the tooth's surface, and the type and form of teeth. Individuals with xerostomia (a failure to form saliva) often exhibit rampant dental caries. In most people, however, a flow of saliva bathes tooth surfaces and clears carbohydrates from the oral cavity.

(6). The chemical nature of the tooth's surface also plays a key role in determining susceptibility to dental caries and the ultimate course of the disease. Surface application of fluoride, for example, can reduce the solubility of the enamel. The fluoride ion inhibits the progress of caries by replacing hydroxyl ions in the hydroxylapatite to form fluorapatite, aiding in the remineralization of the carious lesion by promoting the deposition of calcium phosphate.

(7). The frequency of dental caries varies with the different types and positions of teeth. Interproximal surfaces (the tooth's surfaces that oppose neighboring teeth) are prime sites for the initiation of caries, especially in the contact areas. The teeth that are least susceptible to dental caries are the mandibular central and lateral incisors.

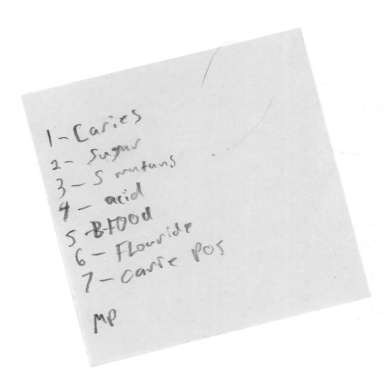

11. The main point of this passage is that

    A.   a dietary intake high in refined carbohydrates causes dental caries.
    B.   the mouth represents a complex microenvironment affected by a variety of physiochemical processes.
    C.   the development of dental caries is a complex process involving bacteria and the host's oral cavity and teeth.
    D.   dental caries should be clinically recognized during early biochemical stages.
    E.   there are mechanisms by which dental caries can be prevented.

12. The initial event leading to the development of dental caries is

    A.   invasion of the oral cavity by pathogenic bacteria.
    B.   the direct adherence of bacterial dextrans to the tooth's enamel.
    C.   the dissolution of inorganic ions.
    D.   the formation of plaque on enamel.
    E.   the production of proteolytic enzymes.

13. Dental caries is least likely to occur in

    A.   interproximal surfaces.
    B.   areas in which teeth contact each other.
    C.   lateral incisors.
    D.   individuals with no salivary flow.
    E.   between the bicuspids.

14. A throbbing pain associated with the eating of ice cream most likely indicates that a carious lesion has begun to

    A.   involve a tooth's pulp.
    B.   affect the individual's systemic health.
    C.   inflame a tooth's dentin.
    D.   dissolve the inorganic structure of a tooth's enamel.
    E.   destroy the minerals in tooth enamel.

15. A recent immigrant from a third-world country visits the dentist. Based on the information in the passage, the dentist would most likely NOT see

   A. damage to enamel caused by carbohydrate consumption.
   B. a high incidence of dental caries.
   C. a failure to form saliva.
   D. tooth damage caused by lack of fluoride in the diet.
   E. mandibular central incisors particularly susceptible to dental caries.

16. Dentin is the primary barrier to the development of dental caries, because decreasing the solubility of dentin by the application of fluoride ions can reduce susceptibility.

   A. Both the statement and the reason are correct and related.
   B. Both the statement and the reason are correct but NOT related.
   C. The statement is correct, but the reason is NOT.
   D. The statement is NOT correct, but the reason is correct.
   E. NEITHER the statement NOR the reason is correct.

17. The author clearly believes that

   A. scientific experiments involving dental caries largely have been unsuccessful.
   B. patients with poor hygiene deserve to have dental caries.
   C. national fluoridation programs have largely been successful.
   D. a number of complex factors influence the frequency and course of dental caries.
   E. understanding dental caries helps patients to prevent caries from forming.

18. Microorganisms attach to salivary proteins via dextrans in their extracellular coats. *Streptococcus aureus* is an example of a microorganism that causes dental caries.

   A. Both statements are true.
   B. Both statements are false.
   C. The first statement is true, the second is false.
   D. The first statement is false, the second is true.

Study Plan

After Class: Reading Comprehension 1

Complete Remaining *Lesson Book* Practice Questions	30m	

Before Class: Biology 1

Read *Review Notes* Chapters 4–9, 19–21	4h 30m	
Generalized Eukaryotic Cell Workshop	45m	
Molecular Genetics Workshop	45m	

- Read Strategically
- use Keywords
- Stop and think
- predict

BIOLOGY 1

TOPICS COVERED

- The Survey of Natural Sciences Section
- The Biology Subsection
- Diversity of Life
- Cell and Molecular Biology
- Genetics
- Evolution, Ecology, and Behavior

After this session you will be able to:

- Differentiate between the taxonomy kingdoms
- Describe the parts of a cell, including their origins and functions
- Explain the processes of replication, transcription, and translation
- Calculate individual and population genetics
- Describe relationships among different organisms and environments

The Survey of Natural Sciences Section

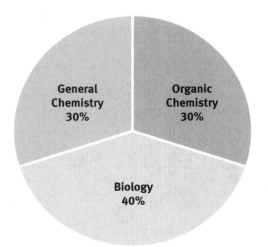

**The distribution of Survey of
Natural Sciences questions**

Overview

- 100 questions in 90 minutes
- Consists of 40 Biology questions, 30 General Chemistry questions, and 30 Organic Chemistry questions
- Allows for use of a Periodic Table of the Elements, accessible by clicking the "Exhibit" button
- No calculator will be available during any part of the Survey of Natural Sciences

The Biology Subsection

Overview

- 40 questions (40% of the Survey of Natural Sciences section)

Topics

Cell and Molecular Biology

- Cellular Structure and Processes
- Organelle Structure and Function
- Cell Metabolism
- Thermodynamics
- Photosynthesis
- Mitosis and Meiosis
- Origin of Life
- Experimental Cell Biology

Developmental Biology

- Fertilization
- Descriptive Embryology
- Developmental Mechanisms

Genetics

- Molecular Genetics
- Human Genetics
- Classical Genetics
- Chromosomal Genetics
- Genetic Technology

Evolution, Ecology, and Behavior

- Natural Selection
- Speciation
- Population and Community Ecology
- Ecosystems
- Animal Behavior

Diversity of Life

- Eubacteria
- Archaea
- Plantae
- Animalia
- Protista
- Fungi
- Relationships

Anatomy and Physiology

- Integumentary
- Skeletal
- Muscular
- Circulatory
- Immunological
- Digestive
- Respiratory
- Urinary
- Nervous
- Endocrine
- Reproductive

The Kaplan Question Strategy

STOP

➜ Characterize the answer choices.

THINK

➜ What is the question really asking?

➜ What relevant information do you need?

PREDICT

➜ Formulate a framework or prediction for your answer.

MATCH

➜ Select the answer that truly meets the requirements of the prediction.

Diversity of Life

Six-Kingdom, Three-Domain System

Bacteria Domain

Eubacteria Kingdom

Archaea Domain

Archaea Kingdom

Eukarya Domain

Protista Kingdom

Fungi Kingdom

Plantae Kingdom

Animalia Kingdom

Cell and Molecular Biology

Origin of Life

Early Conditions

Primordial Soup

First Biological Molecules

Coacervate Droplets

Chemoautotrophs

Aerobes

Practice Questions

1. Suppose you find a previously unidentified, multicellular species with cells containing a nucleus, membrane-bound organelles, and a rigid cell wall but no cellulose. Based on this information alone, which kingdom is the best fit for this species?

   A. Eubacteria
   B. Plantae
   C. Animalia
   D. Protista
   E. Fungi

2. Platyhelminthes are members of the kingdom

   A. Archaea.
   B. Plantae.
   C. Animalia.
   D. Protista.
   E. Fungi.

3. Which of the following free elements was likely most essential to the first life on earth?

   A. Sulfur
   B. Iron
   C. Oxygen
   D. Phosphorus
   E. Calcium

Cell Structure

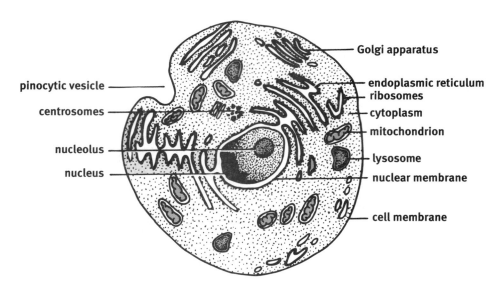

pinocytic vesicle —
centrosomes —
nucleolus —
nucleus —

Golgi apparatus
endoplasmic reticulum
ribosomes
cytoplasm
mitochondrion
lysosome
nuclear membrane
cell membrane

Components

Nucleus

Endoplasmic Reticulum

Ribosome

Golgi Apparatus

Mitochondrion

Lysosome

Cell Processes

Plasma Membrane

Cellular Transport

 Diffusion

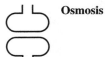 **Osmosis**

 Facilitated Diffusion

 Active Transport

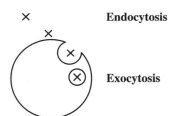 **Endocytosis**

Exocytosis

Practice Questions

4. Autophagy, the degradation of unnecessary cellular components, is most likely dependent on which organelle?

    A.   Ribosome

    B.   Chloroplast

    C.   Lysosome

    D.   Golgi apparatus

    E.   Rough endoplasmic reticulum

5. All of the following statements describe a mitochondrion EXCEPT one. Which statement is the EXCEPTION?

    A.   It contains double-stranded, circular DNA.

    B.   It contains its own ribosomes.

    C.   It is a two-membrane structure.

    D.   It is directly involved in carbohydrate synthesis.

    E.   It replicates by binary fission.

6. Which one of the following statements most accurately describes a process of membrane traffic?

    A.   Active transport requires energy in the form of NADPH.

    B.   Facilitated diffusion requires a carbohydrate carrier.

    C.   Osmosis is the passive transport of nonpolar molecules.

    D.   Endocytosis is an active transport process that moves large volumes of substances into the cell.

    E.   Diffusion is the movement of molecules from lower to higher concentration.

Practice Questions

7. What happens to an ocean (saltwater) fish after it moves into a river (fresh water)?

   A.   Water flows into the fish, causing its cells to lyse.

   B.   Water flows out of the fish, causing its cells to become flaccid.

   C.   Ions flow into the fish, causing the fish to become hypertonic relative to its environment.

   D.   Ions flow out of the fish, causing the fish to become hypertonic relative to its environment.

   E.   No change occurs.

8. You set up a container separated into two compartments by a membrane permeable to water but not ions and then add 1.5 M NaCl to the left compartment and 2.0 M glucose to the right compartment, causing

   A.   water to flow into the left compartment.

   B.   water to flow into the right compartment.

   C. Na^+ and Cl^- to flow into the left compartment.

   D. Na^+ and Cl^- to flow into the right compartment.

   E. Na^+ but not Cl^- to flow into the right compartment.

9. The sodium potassium pump is an ATPase that pumps 3 Na^+ out of the cell and 2 K^+ into the cell for each ATP hydrolyzed. Cells can use the pump to help maintain cell volume. Which of the following would most likely happen to the rate of ATP consumption immediately after a cell is moved to a hypotonic environment?

   A.   It would increase.

   B.   It would decrease.

   C.   It would increase and then decrease.

   D.   It would decrease and then increase.

   E.   It would remain the same.

Cell Metabolism

ATP

adenine

triphosphate group

high-energy bonds

ribose

Glycolysis

Anaerobic Metabolism

Fermentation

Aerobic Metabolism

Pyruvate Decarboxylation

Krebs Cycle (Citric Acid Cycle)

Electron Transport Chain/Oxidative Phosphorylation

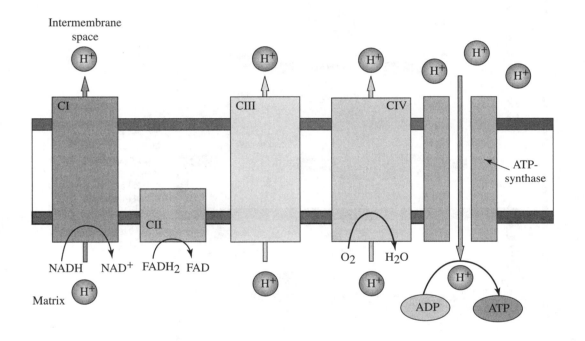

Thermodynamics

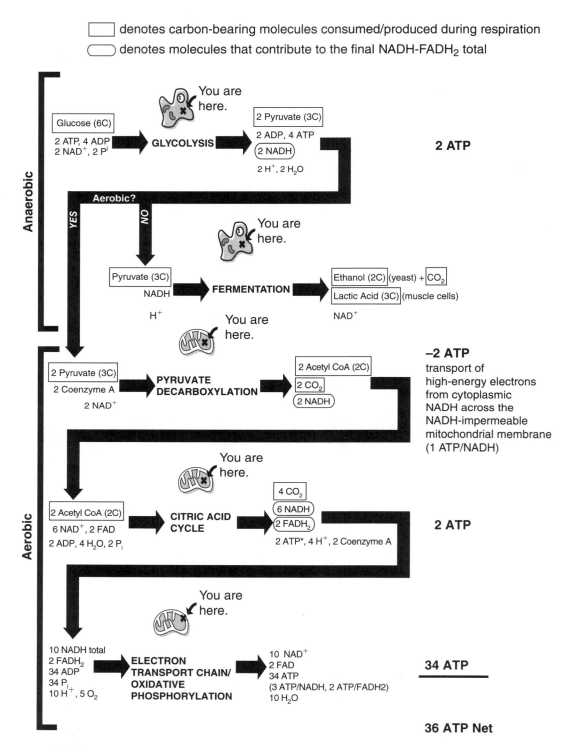

☐ denotes carbon-bearing molecules consumed/produced during respiration

⬭ denotes molecules that contribute to the final NADH-FADH$_2$ total

Anaerobic

Glucose (6C)

2 ATP, 4 ADP
2 NAD$^+$, 2 P^i

GLYCOLYSIS

You are here.

2 Pyruvate (3C)

2 ADP, 4 ATP
(2 NADH)

2 H$^+$, 2 H$_2$O

2 ATP

Aerobic?

YES

NO

Pyruvate (3C)

NADH

H$^+$

FERMENTATION

You are here.

Ethanol (2C) (yeast) + CO$_2$

Lactic Acid (3C) (muscle cells)

NAD$^+$

Aerobic

You are here.

2 Pyruvate (3C)

2 Coenzyme A

2 NAD$^+$

PYRUVATE DECARBOXYLATION

2 Acetyl CoA (2C)

(2 CO$_2$)

(2 NADH)

−2 ATP

transport of
high-energy electrons
from cytoplasmic
NADH across the
NADH-impermeable
mitochondrial membrane
(1 ATP/NADH)

You are here.

2 Acetyl CoA (2C)

6 NAD$^+$, 2 FAD
2 ADP, 4 H$_2$O, 2 P$_i$

CITRIC ACID CYCLE

4 CO$_2$

(6 NADH)

(2 FADH$_2$)

2 ATP*, 4 H$^+$, 2 Coenzyme A

2 ATP

You are here.

10 NADH total
2 FADH$_2$
34 ADP
34 P$_i$
10 H$^+$, 5 O$_2$

ELECTRON TRANSPORT CHAIN/ OXIDATIVE PHOSPHORYLATION

10 NAD$^+$
2 FAD
34 ATP
(3 ATP/NADH, 2 ATP/FADH2)
10 H$_2$O

34 ATP

36 ATP Net

*2 GTP are the direct products of the citric acid cycle. The 2 GTP subsequently
donate their phosphate to 2 ADP to form 2 ATP and regenerate the original 2 GDP.

Practice Questions

10. Which one of the following statements accurately describes cellular metabolism?

    A. Alcohol produced during fermentation undergoes glycolysis to produce 2 ATP.
    B. $FADH_2$ molecules yield three ATP each during oxidative phosphorylation.
    C. Pyruvate decarboxylation directly produces 2 net ATP.
    D. Glycolysis cannot occur in the absence of oxygen.
    E. Oxidative phosphorylation takes place across the inner mitochondrial membrane.

11. What is the last enzyme used during cellular respiration?

    A. Hexokinase
    B. Pyruvate decarboxylase
    C. Alcohol dehydrogenase
    D. Cytochrome C oxidase
    E. Phosphoglucose isomerase

12. The complete absence of which of the following substrates would NOT be expected to limit the rate of oxidative phosphorylation?

    A. NAD^+
    B. H^+
    C. O_2
    D. $FADH_2$
    E. Inorganic phosphate

Photosynthesis

Leaf Anatomy

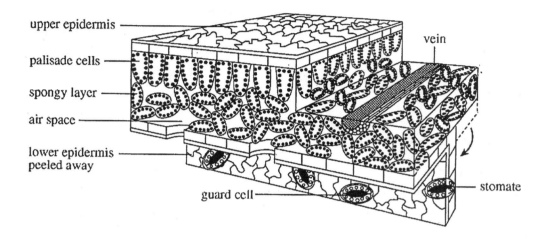

upper epidermis

palisade cells

spongy layer

air space

lower epidermis
peeled away

guard cell

vein

stomate

Upper Epidermis

Cuticle

Mesophyll

Chloroplasts

Thylakoids

Stroma

Lower Epidermis

Stomata

Guard cells

Veins

Xylem

Phloem

Reactions

$$3 CO_2 + 3 H_2O + \text{light energy} \rightarrow C_3H_6O_3 + 3 O_2$$

Light Reaction

Chlorophyll captures light energy from the sun to generate high-energy molecules.

$$6 H_2O + 6 NADP^+ + 9 ADP + 9 P_i + \text{light energy} \rightarrow 6 NADPH + 6 H^+ + 9 ATP + 3 O_2$$

Calvin Cycle (Dark Reaction)

RuBP captures CO_2 from the environment to generate PGAL.

$$3 CO_2 + 9 ATP + 6 NADPH + 6 H^+ \rightarrow C_3H_6O_3 + 3 H_2O + 6 NADP^+ + 9 ADP + 8 P_i$$

Practice Questions

13. In plants, the Calvin cycle of photosynthesis takes place within the

    A. cuticle.
    B. grana.
    C. stroma.
    D. stomata.
    E. xylem.

14. How many total PGAL must be produced for a plant to create one sucrose molecule ($C_{12}H_{22}O_{11}$)?

    A. 4
    B. 6
    C. 12
    D. 24
    E. 30

15. During a drought, a plant may adapt in all of the following ways EXCEPT one. Which is the EXCEPTION?

    A. Allowing its leaves and stems to turn brown
    B. Expanding its root system
    C. Changing concentrations of solutes within its phloem
    D. Slowing or halting its rate of photosynthesis
    E. Opening additional stomata within its leaves

Enzymology

Enzyme Properties

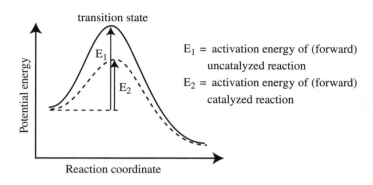

E_1 = activation energy of (forward) uncatalyzed reaction

E_2 = activation energy of (forward) catalyzed reaction

Factors that Affect Enzymes

Temperature

pH

Cofactors/Coenzymes

Concentrations of Substrate and Enzyme

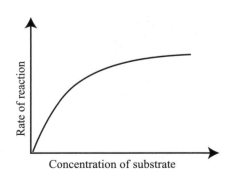

Inhibition

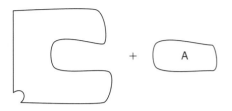

Competitive

Noncompetitive

Negative Feedback

Practice Questions

16. Which set of graphs best depicts the optimal temperature and pH range for pepsin activity?

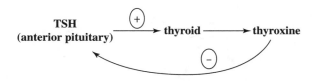

17. In the diagram below, what role does thyroxine play?

TSH
(anterior pituitary) ——(+)——> thyroid ———> thyroxine
                        (-)

   A.   It reduces enzyme specificity.
   B.   It triggers a positive feedback loop.
   C.   It stimulates catalyst production.
   D.   It triggers a negative feedback loop.
   E.   It serves as a substrate for further reaction.

18. An enzyme is introduced into a reaction for which the reactants are substrates to that enzyme. Which of the following occurs?

   A.   The rate at which the equilibrium is reached is increased.
   B.   The equilibrium point is shifted forward.
   C.   The activation energy is increased.
   D.   The free energy of the reaction is increased.
   E.   The equilibrium point is shifted backward.

Genetics

Molecular Genetics

DNA Structure

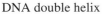

DNA double helix

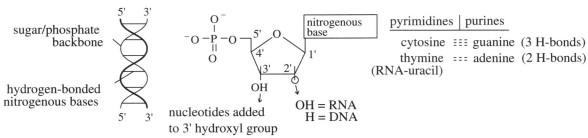

sugar/phosphate backbone

hydrogen-bonded nitrogenous bases

nucleotides added to 3' hydroxyl group

OH = RNA
H = DNA

pyrimidines	purines
cytosine $\equiv$ guanine (3 H-bonds)	
thymine $=$ adenine (2 H-bonds)	
(RNA-uracil)	

DNA Replication

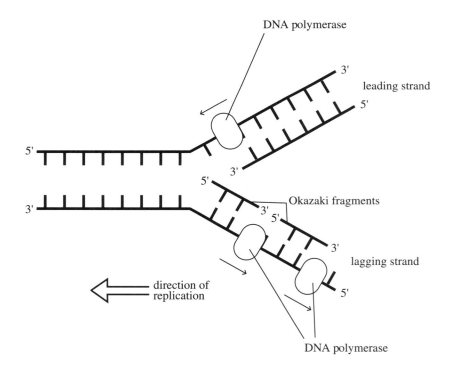

DNA polymerase

leading strand

Okazaki fragments

lagging strand

direction of replication

DNA polymerase

Practice Questions

19. Which daughter strand is more likely to have a mutation?

    A.   The leading strand; more molecules dock and exit during the creation of this strand as compared to the lagging strand.

    B.   The lagging strand; more molecules dock and exit during the creation of this strand as compared to the leading strand.

    C.   The leading strand; fewer molecules dock and exit during the creation of this strand as compared to the lagging strand.

    D.   The lagging strand; fewer molecules dock and exit during the creation of this strand as compared to the leading strand.

    E.   Neither strand; the same number of molecules dock and exit during the creation of both strands.

20. You have two fragments of DNA: Fragment A melts (comes apart) at 97°C, and fragment B melts at 65°C. What can you conclude about the two fragments with respect to their nucleotide composition?

    A.   Fragment A contains more guanine than fragment B.

    B.   Fragment B contains more cytosine than fragment A.

    C.   Fragment A contains more thymine than fragment B.

    D.   Fragment B contains less adenine than fragment A.

    E.   Fragment A contains less uracil than fragment B.

21. What gives a molecule of DNA its negative charge?

    A.   The nitrogenous bases

    B.   The ribose sugar

    C.   The presence of cytosine or thymine

    D.   The hydroxyl group

    E.   The phosphate group

Differences between DNA and RNA in Humans

	DNA	RNA
Base pairs		
Single- or double-stranded		
Functions		

Three Types of RNA

mRNA: messenger RNA; codes for amino acids

tRNA: transfer RNA; brings amino acids to ribosome

rRNA: ribosomal RNA; component of ribosome

Process of Transcription

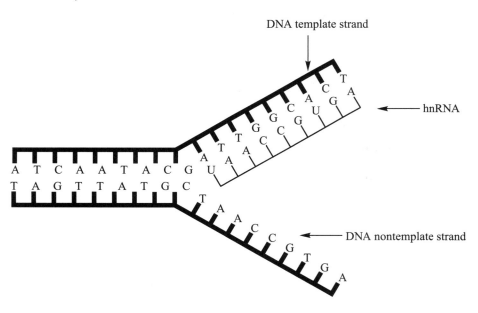

Post-Transcriptional RNA Processing

Practice Questions

22. A segment of a DNA strand has the base sequence 5'—GTTCATTG—3'. What would be the base sequence of the mRNA strand transcribed from this DNA?

   A.   5'—CAATGAAC—3'
   B.   5'—GTTCATTG—3'
   C.   5'—CAAUGAAC—3'
   D.   5'—ACCGUCCA—3'
   E.   5'—CAAGUAAC—3'

23. A person has a mutation in the promoter site of the gene for the lactase enzyme, rendering the promoter site nonfunctional. What symptom(s) will occur?
   I.   Less digestion of lactose by the person
   II.   More digestion of lactose by the person's symbiotic gut bacteria
   III.   Malnutrition due to glucose deficiency

   A.   I
   B.   II
   C.   I and II
   D.   I and III
   E.   I, II, and III

24. Researchers measure the concentration of RNA found in a set of cells for a particular gene and find it to be elevated. What must be occurring in the cells?

   A.   The cells are erythrocytes responding to an oxygen deficit.
   B.   The cells are leukocytes responding to an infection.
   C.   A signal has been received by these cells to upregulate the translation of the gene.
   D.   A signal has been received by these cells to downregulate the replication of the gene.
   E.   A signal has been received by these cells to upregulate the transcription of the gene.

Translation

Three Stages

- Initiation

- Elongation

- Termination

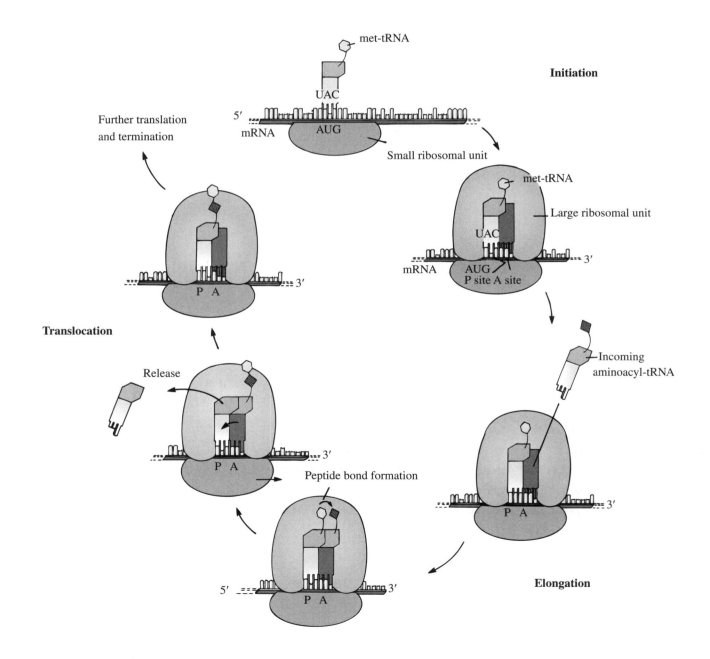

met-tRNA

Initiation

UAC

5′

Further translation
and termination

mRNA AUG

Small ribosomal unit

met-tRNA

Large ribosomal unit

UAC

mRNA 3′

AUG
P site A site

Incoming
aminoacyl-tRNA

Translocation

P A 3′

Release

P A 3′

Peptide bond formation

P A 3′

P A 3′

5′

Elongation

5′ P A 3′

Practice Questions

25. What would happen if a tRNA with an anti-codon for alanine was actually carrying the amino acid valine?

   A. An alanine would be added where a valine was coded for during translation.
   B. A valine would be added where an alanine was coded for during translation.
   C. No amino acid would be added for that codon during translation.
   D. Both an alanine and a valine would be added at that codon during translation.
   E. Translation would immediately stop if the tRNA was to bind to the ribosome complex.

26. A new type of antibiotic targets and destroys bacterial ribosomes. How does this antibiotic work?

   A. Bacteria die because they can no longer synthesize plasmids.
   B. Bacteria die because they can no longer synthesize lipids.
   C. Bacteria die because they can no longer synthesize carbohydrates.
   D. Bacteria die because they can no longer synthesize proteins.
   E. Bacteria die because they can no longer synthesize nucleic acids.

27. A mutation causes peptidyl transferase to be nonfunctional. What process would this halt?

   A. Ribosome assembly
   B. tRNA anticodons recognizing mRNA codons
   C. Peptide bond formation
   D. Binding between rRNA and mRNA
   E. None of the above

Mutations

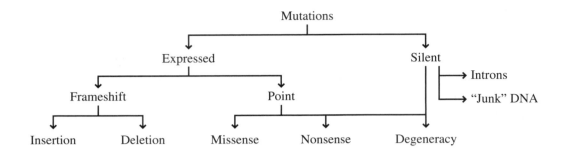

Point Mutation

Silent Mutation

Missense Mutation

Nonsense Mutation

Frameshift Mutation

Chromosomal Mutation

    Turner Syndrome

    Klinefelter Syndrome

    Down Syndrome

Practice Questions

28. What must happen for a mutation to be noticeable in a human?

    A. The mutation is a point mutation.
    B. The mutation changes one amino acid to another.
    C. The mutation is in a region of DNA that is transcribed often.
    D. The mutation is not on a somatic chromosome.
    E. The mutation causes a change in function of a protein.

29. Which of the following mutations is most likely to cause a fetus to be nonviable?

    A. Nonsense
    B. Frameshift
    C. Point
    D. Silent
    E. Chromosomal

30. What causes some point mutations NOT to be expressed?

    I.   The degeneracy of the amino acid codon code
    II.   If the point mutation is in the second position of the codon
    III. The concept of "wobble" in the codon code

    A. I
    B. II
    C. I and III
    D. II and III
    E. I, II, and III

Classical Genetics

Punnett Square

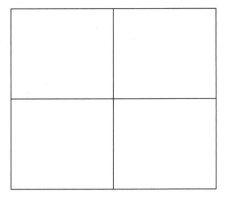

Phenotypic and Genotypic Ratios

Monohybrid Cross

Dihybrid Cross

Human Genetics

Autosomal Recessive Pedigree

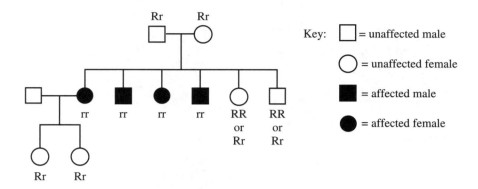

Autosomal Dominant Pedigree

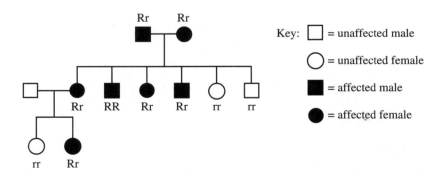

X-Linked Recessive Pedigree

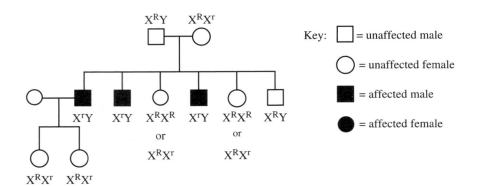

TAKEAWAY

When tackling pedigree questions, focus on the specific patterns rather than wasting time by mapping all of the genotypes.

Practice Questions

31. Given the pedigree below, what is the likelihood the offspring is a carrier?

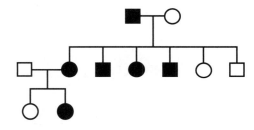

A. 25%

B. 50%

C. 66%

D. 75%

E. 100%

32. What is the inheritance pattern of the observed trait indicated by the pedigree below?

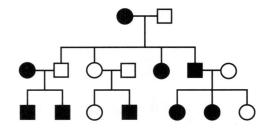

A. Autosomal recessive

B. Autosomal dominant

C. X-linked recessive

D. Y-linked

E. Cannot be determined

33. What is the inheritance pattern of the observed trait indicated by the pedigree below?

A. Autosomal recessive

B. Autosomal dominant

C. X-linked recessive

D. X-linked dominant

E. Cannot be determined

Evolution, Ecology, and Behavior

Evolution

Natural Selection

Patterns of Evolution

Divergent

Convergent

Parallel

Coevolution

Population Genetics

Hardy-Weinberg Conditions

1. Random Mating

2. No Natural Selection

3. No Migration or Emigration

4. Large Population

5. No Mutations

Hardy-Weinberg Equations

$(p + q)^n = 1$

$p + q = 1$

$p^2 + 2pq + q^2 = 1$

Practice Questions

34. If 84% of the population has Rh⁺ blood, which is coded for by a dominant allele, then what is the frequency of the recessive allele, assuming Hardy-Weinberg equilibrium?

  A. 8.3%
  B. 16%
  C. 40%
  D. 60%
  E. 92%

35. Red hair, a recessive trait, appears in only 1% of the world's population. Assuming no source of evolution is occurring, what is the frequency of the allele for red hair?

  A. 0.1%
  B. 1%
  C. 2%
  D. 10%
  E. 20%

36. Some plants, such as cotton and potatoes, are tetraploid (4*n*). If a recessive allele q has a frequency of 0.20 for a certain population of tetraploid plants in equilibrium, what is the frequency of the homozygous recessive genotype of qqqq?

  A. 0.16%
  B. 0.80%
  C. 4.0%
  D. 8.0%
  E. 16%

K

Practice Questions

37. Sharks, which are a type of fish, and dolphins, which are a type of mammal, share similar, torpedo-shaped body plans with fins. This is most likely due to

    A.   divergent evolution.
    B.   convergent evolution.
    C.   the founder effect.
    D.   speciation.
    E.   vestigial structures.

38. On a certain island, one bird species faces heavy competition for a sole food source. If a mutation is introduced that leads to exploitation of a new food source and eventually speciation, what type of evolution occurred?

    A.   Divergent evolution
    B.   Convergent evolution
    C.   Coevolution
    D.   Sexual selection
    E.   Parallel evolution

39. The wings of bats and the wings of birds can be considered

    A.   vestigial structures.
    B.   homologous traits.
    C.   analogous traits.
    D.   comparative embryology evidence for evolution.
    E.   comparative biochemistry evidence for evolution.

Ecosystems

Terrestrial Biomes

Freshwater Biomes

Marine Biomes

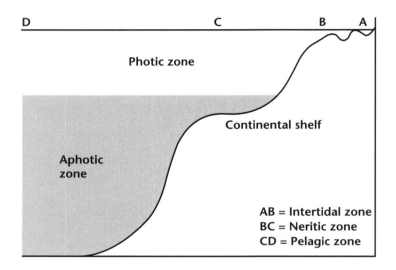

Ecological Succession

Pioneer Organisms

Climax Community

Community Ecology

Commensalism

Mutualism

Parasitism

Predation

Animal Behavior

Classical Conditioning

Operant Conditioning

Behavioral Displays

Pecking Order

Territoriality

Pheromones

Practice Questions

40. A biome with thin soil that contains significant populations of pines, spruces, bison, and beaver is best characterized as

   A.   coniferous forest.
   B.   grassland.
   C.   rainforest.
   D.   taiga.
   E.   tundra.

41. Which of the following species is most likely to be found as a permanent resident of the intertidal zone?

   A.   Hammerhead shark
   B.   Stingray
   C.   Seagull
   D.   Tuna
   E.   Mussel

42. After a lichen has settled a barren rock, the next species to settle is most likely to be a

   A.   pine tree.
   B.   blueberry shrub.
   C.   mountain moss.
   D.   scrub hare.
   E.   buffalo grass.

43. The human digestive tract is home to hundreds of species of bacteria. The bacteria are provided with a relatively stable environment, while the host benefits from increased immune function and vitamins as a byproduct of the bacteria. This is an example of

   A.   commensalism.
   B.   mutualism.
   C.   brood parasitism.
   D.   obligate parasitism.
   E.   predation.

PERCEPTUAL ABILITY 1

TOPICS COVERED

- The PAT
- Keyholes
- Top-Front-End
- Pattern Folding

After this session you will be able to:

- Recognize the major traits of each PAT subsection
- Recall the specific rules of Keyhole, Top-Front-End, and Pattern Folding questions
- Apply relevant strategies to solve Keyhole, Top-Front-End, and Pattern Folding questions

The PAT

SKIP to 31 and do easy points First

What does this section test?

How does this section test its content?

Timing

60 minutes, 90 questions

The Subsections

15 questions per subsection

Keyholes (12.5 minutes recommended)

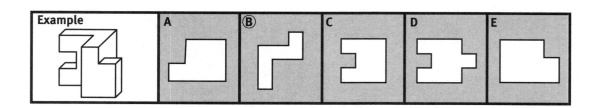

Top-Front-End (12.5 minutes recommended)

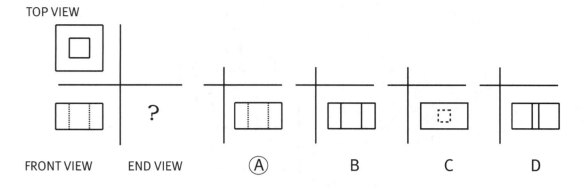

TOP VIEW

FRONT VIEW   END VIEW   Ⓐ   B   C   D

Angle Ranking (5 minutes recommended)

Skip here

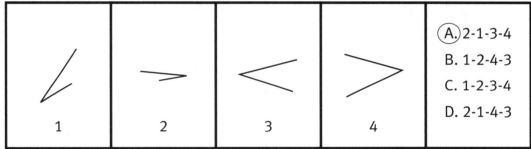

| 1 | 2 | 3 | 4 | Ⓐ A. 2-1-3-4
 B. 1-2-4-3
 C. 1-2-3-4
 D. 2-1-4-3 |

Hole Punching (5 minutes recommended)

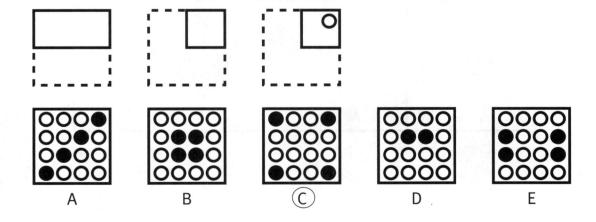

A   B   Ⓒ   D   E

Cube Counting (10 minutes recommended)

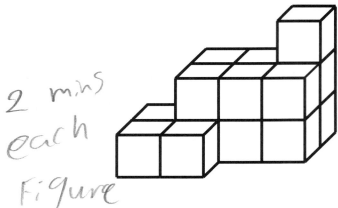

2 mins each figure

How many cubes have one of their sides painted?

3 Qs a figure

A. 1 cube
B. 2 cubes
C. 3 cubes
D. 4 cubes
E. 5 cubes

Pattern Folding (15 minutes recommended)

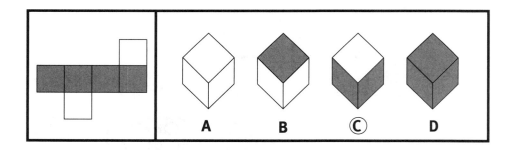

Keyholes

PART 1

For each question, a three-dimensional object is displayed at left. This figure is followed by outlines of five openings or apertures.

The assignment is the same for each question. Imagine how the object at left looks from all directions, not just the one shown. Choose one of the five openings presented that would allow the object to pass through if the proper sides were inserted first.

Basic Rules:

1) The irregular object at left may be rotated in any manner. It may be inserted through the aperture starting with a side not shown.

2) Once the irregular object has started through the aperture, it may not be rotated or turned in any way. The object must pass completely through the aperture. The aperture is always the exact shape of the external outline of the object.

3) Both the irregular object and openings are drawn to the same scale. It is possible that a correct opening may be too small for the object even though it is the proper shape.

4) There are no irregularities in any hidden part of the object. If a figure has symmetric indentations, hidden portions are symmetric with visible parts.

5) There is only one correct answer choice for each object.

Example

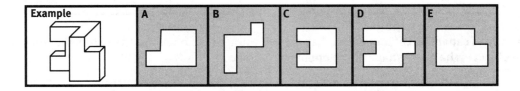

The correct answer is choice (B) since the object would pass through this aperture if the bottom were inserted first.

Proceed to Questions

Overview

Keyholes are the first section of the PAT. A three-dimensional object is presented, and you must determine through which of five openings the object can pass.

The Rules

The object can pass through the opening in any orientation.

Top:

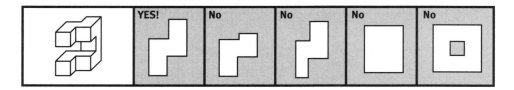

Front:

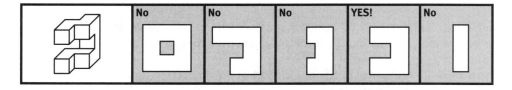

Right:

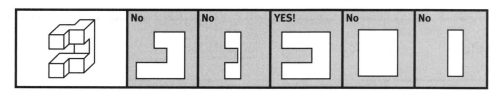

The object cannot be rotated once it has started through the opening. The external outline of the object is the exact shape of the opening.

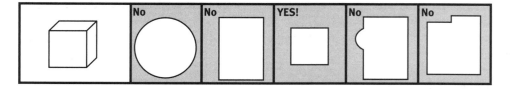

The object and opening are drawn to the same scale.

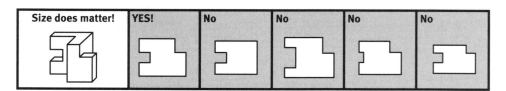

There are no irregularities in any hidden part of the object.

Here is the front of the object . . .   Could this be the back?

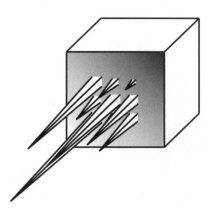

There is only one correct answer.

Strategies

Projections

- Bottom

- Back

- Left

Crushing the Object

Unique Features Elimination

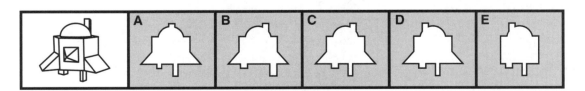

Projections

A projection is a two-dimensional "shadow" of a three-dimensional object.

Examples

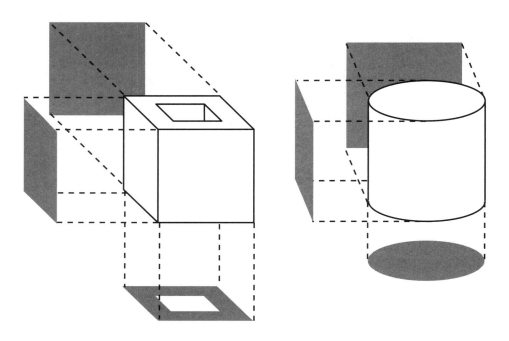

What will a sphere fit through?

What will a pyramid fit through?

Practice with Projections

a.	Draw the back projection here.
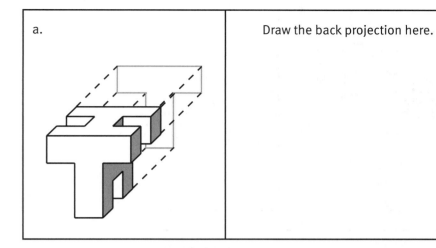	

b.	Draw the bottom projection here.
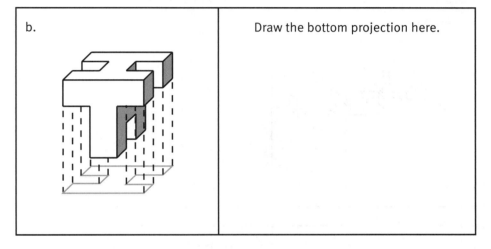	

c.	Draw the left projection here.
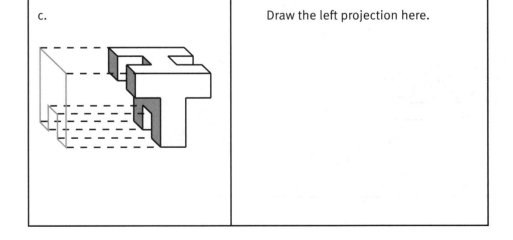	

d.

Draw the back projection here.

e.

Draw the bottom projection here.

f.

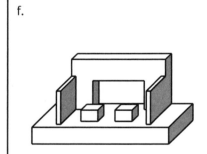

Draw the left projection here.

For the objects below, correctly label the back, bottom, and left projections.

g.

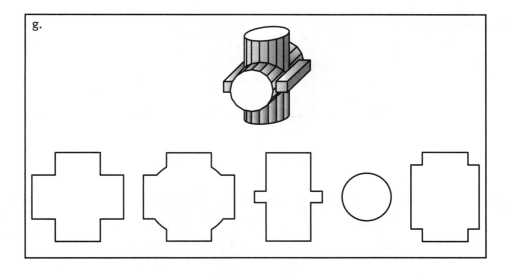

h.

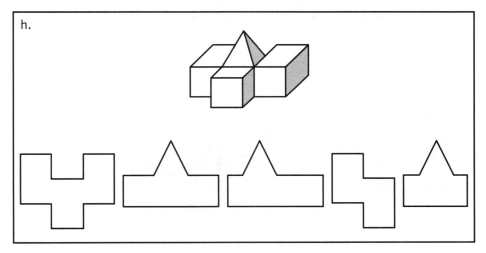

Judging Distance in 3D

i.

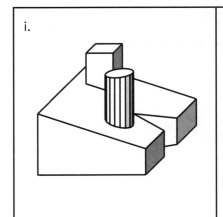

Which is taller: the square column or the circular column?

Is the notch closer to the front, back, or center of the object?

Practice Questions

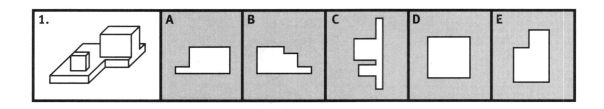

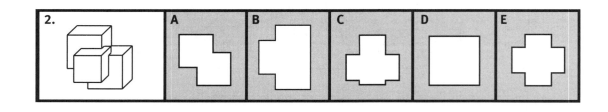

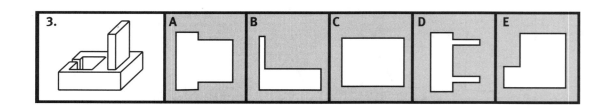

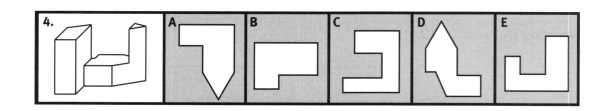

Practice Questions

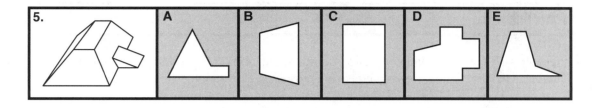

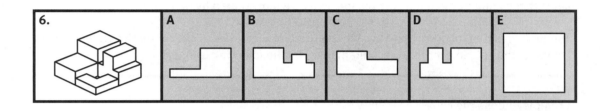

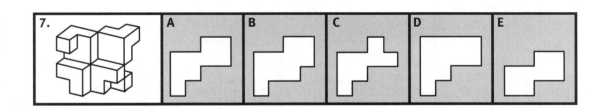

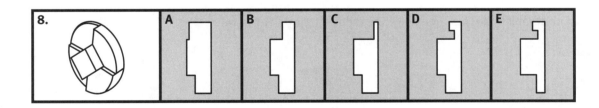

Top-Front-End

PART 2

Presented are top, front, and end views of various solid objects. All views are presented without perspective. Points in the viewed surface are presented along parallel lines of sight.

The TOP VIEW image of the object presents the projection of looking down on the object. The FRONT VIEW image presents a view of the object from the front. The END VIEW illustrates a lateral view of the object from the right. These views are always in the same position.

Lines that cannot be seen in some perspectives are represented by DOTTED lines.

The problems that follow present two views of a particular object. Four alternatives are shown to complete the set. Select the correct alternative. Try the following example:

Example Choose the correct END VIEW.

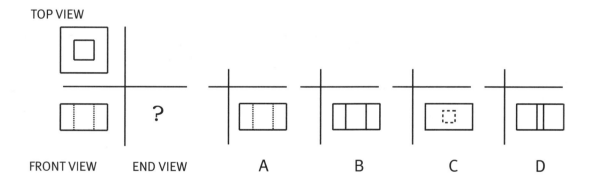

The correct answer is choice (A). The following views are shown:

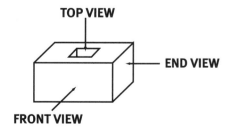

Proceed to Questions

Overview

Two views of an object are presented and you must extrapolate the third.

The Rules

Presented are top, front, and end views of various solid objects.

All objects will be solid, though there can be holes or dents in an object. You won't see an object with another object completely hidden inside of it.

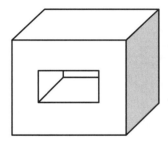

You may see objects like this one, with a hole through the object.

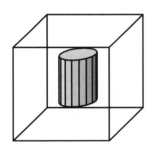

You will not see objects with other objects completely hidden inside.

All views are presented without perspective. Points in the viewed surface are presented along parallel lines of sight.

No Perspective   Perspective

The TOP VIEW, FRONT VIEW, and END VIEW are always presented in the same positions relative to a cross on the left of the page.

Edges of the object that cannot be seen are represented by DOTTED lines.

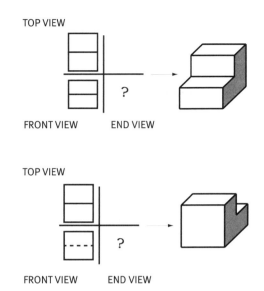

The END VIEW is a lateral view of the object from the right only.

Left vs. Right:

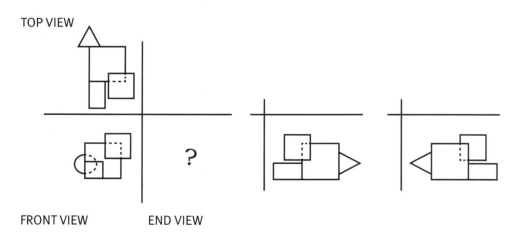

Strategies

Fold the Quadrants

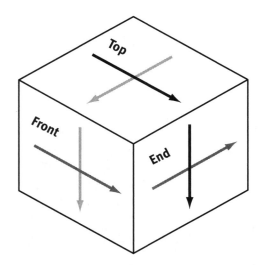

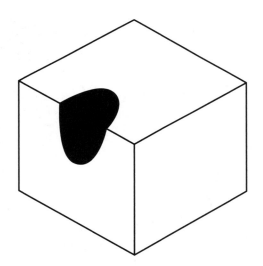

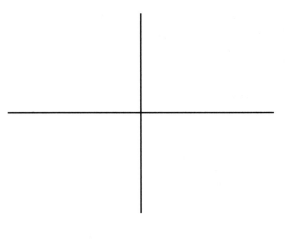

Event Theory

- Angles

- Edges

- Lines

Hidden vs. Visible Events

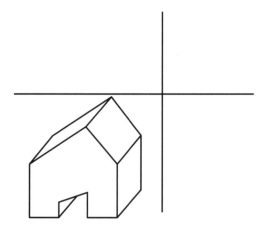

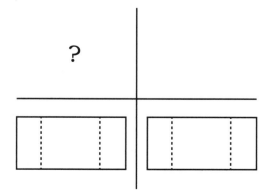

Key Feature/Proportion Elimination

TOP VIEW

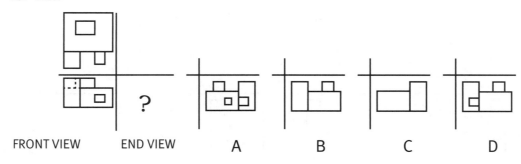

FRONT VIEW   END VIEW   A   B   C   D

TOP VIEW

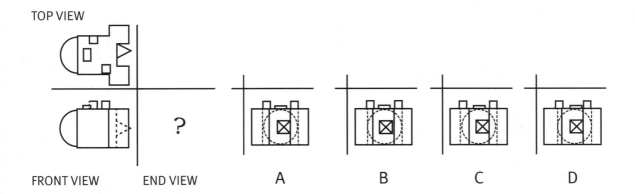

FRONT VIEW   END VIEW   A   B   C   D

Practice Questions

9. Choose the correct **END VIEW**.

TOP VIEW

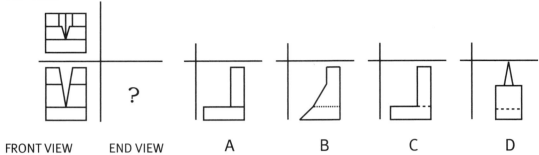

FRONT VIEW   END VIEW   A   B   C   D

10. Choose the correct **TOP VIEW**.

TOP VIEW

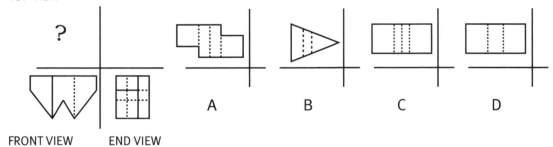

FRONT VIEW   END VIEW   A   B   C   D

11. Choose the correct **END VIEW**.

TOP VIEW

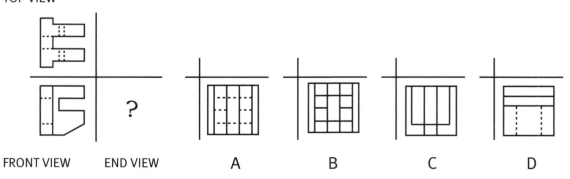

FRONT VIEW   END VIEW   A   B   C   D

Practice Questions

12. Choose the correct **FRONT VIEW**.

TOP VIEW

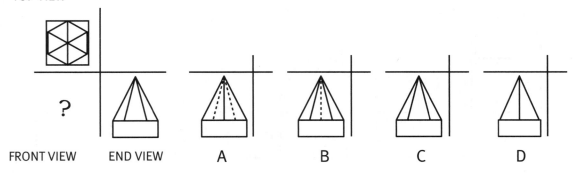

FRONT VIEW   END VIEW   A   B   C   D

13. Choose the correct **FRONT VIEW**.

TOP VIEW

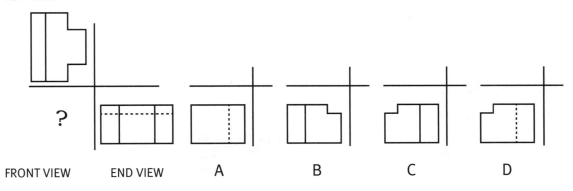

FRONT VIEW   END VIEW   A   B   C   D

14. Choose the correct **FRONT VIEW**.

TOP VIEW

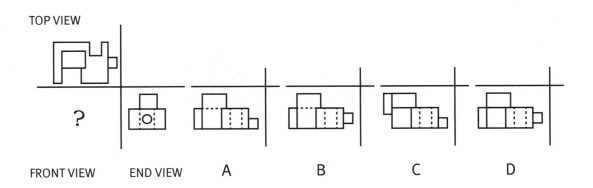

FRONT VIEW   END VIEW   A   B   C   D

Practice Questions

15. Choose the correct **FRONT VIEW.**

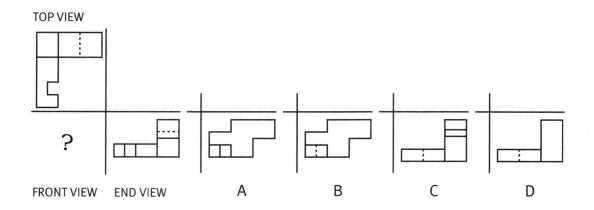

TOP VIEW

FRONT VIEW   END VIEW   A   B   C   D

16. Choose the correct **END VIEW.**

TOP VIEW

FRONT VIEW   END VIEW   A   B   C   D

Top-Front-End 3D Images

9.
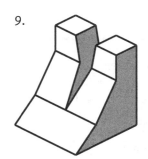

10.
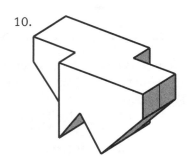

11.
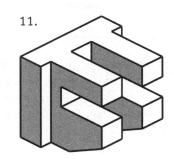

12.
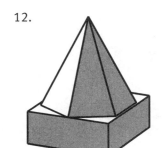

13.
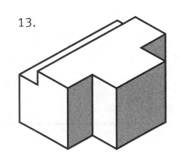

14.
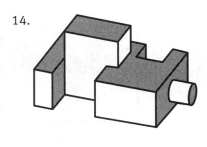

15.
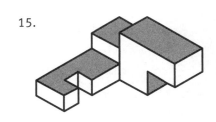

16.
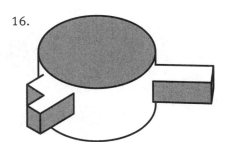

Pattern Folding

PART 6

In the following questions, a flat pattern is presented. This pattern will be folded into a three-dimensional figure, and the correct three-dimensional figure is one of the four answer choices illustrated at the right of the pattern. There is only one correct three-dimensional figure for each question. The pattern at left represents the outside of the figure.

Select the three-dimensional figure that directly corresponds to the pattern at left. Choose the appropriate answer choice. Try the following example:

Example

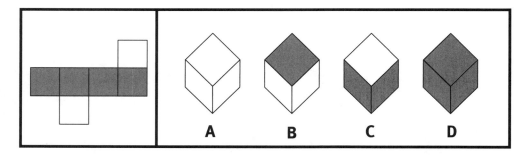

The correct answer is choice (C).

Proceed to Questions

Overview

Determine which three-dimensional shape is produced by folding a two-dimensional pattern.

The Rules

A flat pattern is presented at left.

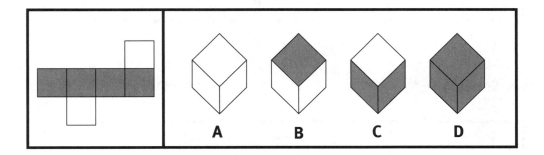

There is only one correct three-dimensional figure for each question.

This means if two choices are different views of the same object, then neither is correct.

The flat pattern represents the *outside* of the figure.

This means the flat pattern must be folded *into the page* in order to produce a three-dimensional object with the pattern facing out.

Strategies

Unique Shape

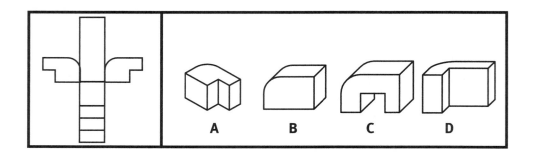

Unique Shading

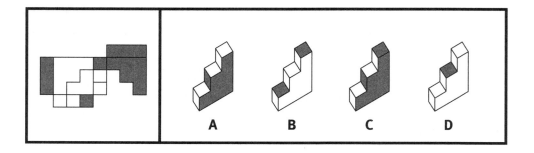

Key Landmark

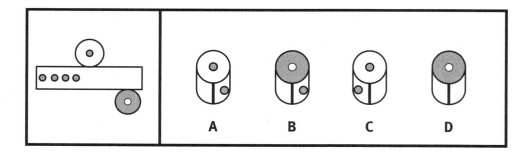

Practice Questions

39.

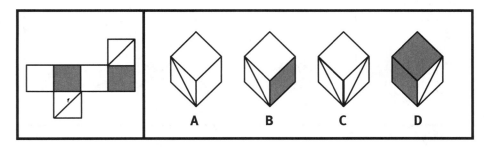

40.

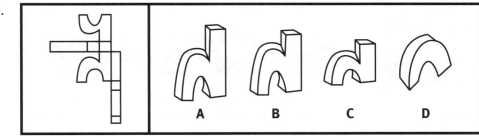

41.

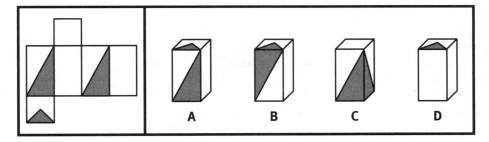

42.

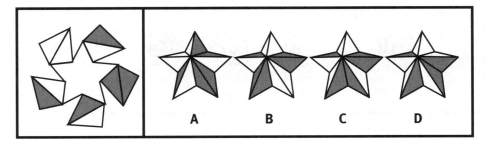

Practice Questions

43.

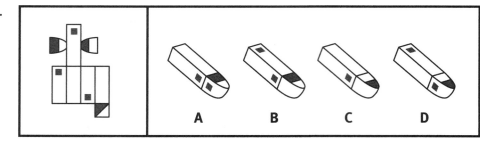

44.

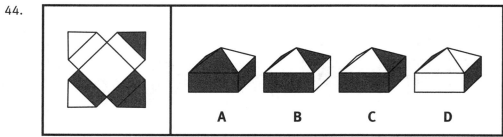

45.

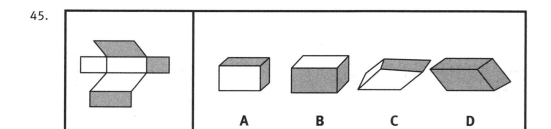

46.

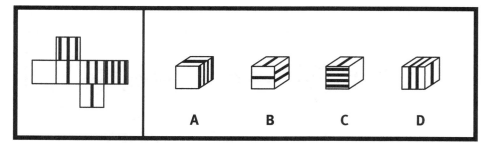

Study Plan

After Class: Perceptual Ability 1

Complete Remaining *Lesson Book* Practice Questions	30m	
Practice with Tests and Quizzes		

Before Class: Quantitative Reasoning 1

Read *Review Notes* Chapters 55–57	1h 30m	
Problem-Solving Basics Workshop	45m	
Number Properties Basics Workshop	45m	
Arithmetic Fundamentals Workshop	45m	
Algebra Basics Workshop	45m	
Graph Basics Workshop	45m	
Fractions Video	5m	
Scientific Notation Video	5m	
Special Question Types Intro	2m	
Quantitative Comparisons Basics Workshop	45m	

QUANTITATIVE REASONING 1

TOPICS COVERED

- The Quantitative Reasoning Section
- Quantitative Reasoning Strategic Overview
- Numerical Calculations
- Algebra

After this session you will be able to:

- Identify opportunities to apply Traditional Math, Picking Numbers, Backsolving, Educated Guessing, and Estimation to math problems
- Solve Quantitative Comparison–style test questions
- Calculate numerical problems involving decimals, exponents, and absolute values
- Calculate algebra problems using equations and inequalities

The Quantitative Reasoning Section

Overview

- 40 questions in 45 minutes

Topics

Numerical Calculations

- Fractions and Decimals
- Percentages
- Approximation
- Scientific Notation

Algebra

- Equations and Expressions
- Inequalities
- Exponential Notation
- Absolute Value
- Ratios and Proportions
- Graphical Analysis

Data Analysis

- Data Interpretation
- Data Sufficiency

Quantitative Comparison

Applied Mathematics (Word) Problems

- Equations and Expressions
- Inequalities
- Exponential Notation
- Absolute Value
- Ratios and Proportions

Conversions

Probability and Statistics

Geometry and Trigonometry

The Kaplan Method for Quantitative Reasoning

STOP

→ Read the question and characterize the answer choices.

THINK

→ What is the question really asking?

→ Pick the strategy to quickly and accurately solve the problem.

- **Picking Numbers:** Use manageable numbers in place of variables.

- **Backsolving:** Plug answers into the question stem.

- **Educated Guessing:** Avoid trap answers.

- **Estimating:** Find a solution close to the correct answer.

- **Traditional Math:** Apply classic math formulas.

PREDICT

→ Use the chosen strategy to formulate a framework or prediction for your answer.

MATCH

→ Select the answer that truly meets the requirements of the prediction.

Quantitative Reasoning Strategic Overview

Picking Numbers

Why Pick Numbers?

- Many people find it easier to perform calculations with numbers than with variables.

When to Pick Numbers

- Percents are in the answer choices.
- Questions that involve number properties.
- Variables are in the answer choices.

How to Pick Numbers

- Pick numbers that are permissible by the rules of the question.
- Pick easy, manageable numbers.
- Avoid numbers with unusual properties, such as one and zero.
- When needed, try sets of numbers that have different properties, such as positives and negatives or odds and evens.

Percentages

Picking numbers works well on percentage questions when the actual values aren't given in the question stem. When picking numbers on a percentage problem, always pick the number 100; this will yield the correct answer more directly.

Example:

1. From June to September, the volume of water held in a certain reservoir fell by 40%. From September to November, the volume of water held by the reservoir increased by 40%. What was the percentage change in volume from June to November?

    A.   A decrease of 80%

    B.   A decrease of 16%

    C.   No change

    D.   An increase of 36%

    E.   An increase of 84%

Number Properties

Picking numbers is especially useful for questions that are abstract or that would be difficult to solve using traditional math, such as those involving number properties (e.g., positive versus negative, odd versus even, factors versus multiples). As with other questions with variables in the answer choices, test your numbers with each answer choice.

Example:

2. If x and y are integers such that $x > y$, which of the following CANNOT be a negative integer?

   A. $y(y - x)$

   B. $y(x - y)$

   C. $x^2 - y$

   D. $\dfrac{(y - x)}{(x - y)}$

   E. $\dfrac{(x - y)}{(y - x)}$

Variables in the Answer Choices

When the answer choices contain variables, consider using Picking Numbers to solve the problem. After choosing numbers, reread the question stem, substituting your numbers for the variables. Finally, plug your numbers into each answer choice.

Example:

3. C individuals pledged to pay equal contributions so that a charity's goal of $\$x$ could be reached. If d of the contributors failed to pay their share, which of the following represents the additional number of dollars that each of the remaining individuals had to pay in order for the charity to reach its goal?

A. $\dfrac{dx}{c}$

B. $\dfrac{x}{c-d}$

C. $\dfrac{d}{c-dx}$

D. $\dfrac{x}{c(c-d)}$

E. $\dfrac{dx}{c(c-d)}$

Backsolving

Backsolving is a quick method to use when the answer choices are numbers. To backsolve, use the answer choices to plug back into the question stem and identify which one works.

Examples:

4. In a class of 7 students, the average score on a test was 80. If 6 of the 7 students scored a 78 on the test, what did the seventh student score?

  A. 85
  B. 88
  C. 90
  D. 92
  E. 95

5. Jacob is 12 years younger than Michael. If, in 9 years, Michael will be twice as old as Jacob, how old is Jacob now?

  A. 3
  B. 7
  C. 9
  D. 12
  E. 15

Estimation

Estimation is useful on problems for which a math formula could solve for the right answer but would take a long time. Estimation saves time and still allows you to get an answer that is close to the correct choice.

Example:

6. What is the approximate sum of 10,485,456 and 650,987,498?

    A. 6.614×10^7
    B. 7.558×10^7
    C. 6.614×10^8
    D. 7.558×10^8
    E. 6.501×10^9

Educated Guessing

Educated Guessing is helpful when a problem is difficult to solve but some of the answer choices can easily be eliminated as incorrect. Educated Guessing can be used to select an answer more accurately before marking and skipping a question and as a safeguard for catching arithmetic mistakes that result in a calculated answer that isn't logically correct.

Example:

7. Esther drove at an average rate of 40 miles per hour for 70 minutes. She then increased her speed to 50 miles per hour and drove for 1 more hour, and then increased her speed to 60 miles per hour and drove for 3 additional hours. What was her average rate, in miles per hour, for the entire trip?

A. 45.5

B. 47.3

C. 51.4

D. 53.5

E. 58.1

Quantitative Reasoning Strategies Summary

Test Day strategy	When to use
Traditional Math	When you know how to set up and answer the problem quickly and efficiently
Picking Numbers	When there are unknown values such as variables in the answer choices or percents with unknown starting values
Backsolving	When the answer choices are numbers that can readily be plugged back into the problem to test which works
Estimation	When the answer choices are relatively far apart and the numbers are awkward and difficult to work with
Educated Guessing	When some of the answer choices can quickly be eliminated; when you don't have enough time to solve the problem; or when you don't know how to solve the problem

TAKEAWAY

Sometimes the best approach for tackling a question is to combine two methods. Determine your approach, then let the methods do the work.

Quantitative Comparisons

Quantitative comparisons are a special type of problem that appear in the Quantitative Reasoning section of the test. Quantitative Comparisons ask you to define the relationship between two numbers, expressions, or statements. There will sometimes be centered information that applies to both columns and that is necessary to determine the relationship between the quantities.

The structure for Quantitative Comparison questions is as follows:

[Optional Centered Information]

Quantity A	Quantity B
Value A	Value B

A. Quantity A is greater.
B. Quantity B is greater.
C. The two quantities are equal.
D. The relationship cannot be determined from the information given.

Because the answers to Quantitative Comparisons are about relationships, it is not always necessary to calculate exact values. Instead, find ways to compare the values in the columns.

Examples:

8.

Quantity A	Quantity B
$\frac{1}{7} + \frac{1}{8} + \frac{1}{9}$	$\frac{3}{10}$

A. Quantity A is greater.
B. Quantity B is greater.
C. The two quantities are equal.
D. The relationship cannot be determined from the information given.

9.

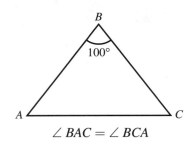

$$\angle BAC = \angle BCA$$

Quantity A	Quantity B
AB	*AC*

A.   Quantity A is greater.

B.   Quantity B is greater.

C.   The two quantities are equal.

D.   The relationship cannot be determined from the information given.

Numerical Calculations

Ratios

Ratios represent the proportion of one quantity to another and can be written as fractions or in the form $c{:}d$.

A ratio does not, by itself, represent the number of each item present.

There are two types of ratios:

- Part-to-whole: numerator or first number is the part; denominator or second number is the whole.
- Part-to-part: both numerator and denominator represent different parts; parts add up to the whole.

Example:

10. What is the ratio of the average score of Class A to the average score of Class B on a test if the scores are as follows?

Students	Scores
Student 1 (Class A)	76
Student 2 (Class A)	90
Student 3 (Class A)	85
Student 4 (Class B)	66
Student 5 (Class B)	95
Student 6 (Class B)	87

    A. $\dfrac{25}{26}$

    B. $\dfrac{251}{248}$

    C. $\dfrac{85}{80}$

    D. $\dfrac{250}{227}$

    E. $\dfrac{91}{81}$

Practice Questions

11. At a floral shop, the rules require that all flower arrangements have 6 daisies for every 3 roses and 2 lilies for every 4 daisies. If a floral arrangement has one dozen roses, how many daises and lilies must also be present?

    A.   4 lilies and 8 daisies
    B.   6 lilies and 12 daisies
    C.   12 lilies and 24 daisies
    D.   9 lilies and 18 daisies
    E.   6 lilies and 24 daisies

12. If $x = \dfrac{1}{y} = 2$, what is the ratio of x^4 to y^4?

    A. $\dfrac{1}{16}$

    B. $\dfrac{1}{2}$

    C. $\dfrac{1}{1}$

    D. $\dfrac{32}{1}$

    E. $\dfrac{256}{1}$

13.
$$\frac{a}{b} > \frac{c}{b}$$

b is not equal to 0

Quantity A	Quantity B
a	c

    A.   Quantity A is greater.
    B.   Quantity B is greater.
    C.   The two quantities are equal.
    D.   The relationship cannot be determined from the information given.

Percentages

Percentage Formulas:

Convert a percent to a decimal by dividing by 100: $\frac{x}{100}$

$$Percent = \frac{Part}{Whole} \times 100\%$$

$$Percent\ Increase = \frac{Final - Original}{Original} \times 100\%$$

As a shortcut to find the percent increase for a value, add the percentage to 100%, convert it to a decimal, and multiply it by the original value.

Example:

A child blows into a balloon originally containing 2 L of gas, causing the volume of the balloon to expand by 30%. What is the new volume of gas in the balloon?

As a shortcut to find the decrease of a number by a percentage, subtract the percentage from 100%, convert it to a decimal, and multiply it by the original value.

Example:

While shopping for bargains, a customer chooses to buy a shirt that originally cost $35, but is on sale for 20% off the original price. How much must the customer now pay for the shirt?

Example:

14. A broker buys $2,500 worth of a certain stock. If the stock price rises by 40% and then falls by 15%, how much would the stock be worth in the end?

    A. $1,375
    B. $2,125
    C. $2,975
    D. $3,125
    E. $3,500

Practice Questions

15. In 1980, the population of a certain district was 9,000 people. The district was divided into two counties: p people lived in County A, and the rest lived in County B. Over the next ten years, the population of County A increased by 9% and the population of County B increased by 5%. By how many people did the population of the entire district increase, in terms of p?

   A. $4p + 45{,}000$
   B. $450 - 0.14p$
   C. $450 + 0.04p$
   D. $-4p + 810$
   E. $810 + 0.04p$

16. Over the course of a year, a certain factory increased its output by 90%. At the same time, it decreased its total working hours by 20%. By what percentage did the factory increase its output per hour?

   A.   70%
   B.   110%
   C.   112.5%
   D.   137.5%
   E.   237.5%

17.   A bicyclist in motion increases his speed by 20%,
                    then increases his speed by another 10%.

   Quantity A   Quantity B

   The bicyclist's final speed   130% of the bicyclist's original speed

   A.   Quantity A is greater.
   B.   Quantity B is greater.
   C.   The two quantities are equal.
   D.   The relationship cannot be determined from the information given.

Algebra

Exponential Notation

A power is a base raised to an exponent.

An example of a power is $3x^2$. In the example, x is the base and 2 is the exponent.

The exponent refers to the number of times the base is a factor in the product.

Exponent Rules

$x^0 = 1$

$x^1 = x$

$x^{-n} = \dfrac{1}{x^n}$

$x^a \cdot x^b = x^{a+b}$

$(x^a)^b = x^{ab}$

$\dfrac{x^a}{x^b} = x^{a-b}$

$(xy)^a = x^a y^a$

$x^{\left(\frac{1}{y}\right)} = \sqrt[y]{x}$

Example:

18. Which of the following is equal to the ratio of $\left(\dfrac{3}{8}\right)^5$ to $\left(\dfrac{3}{8}\right)^6$?

    A. $\dfrac{9}{64}$

    B. $\dfrac{1}{3}$

    C. $\dfrac{3}{8}$

    D. $\dfrac{8}{3}$

    E. 3

Practice Questions

19. If $4^{2x+2} = 16^{3x-1}$, what is the value of x?

    A.   0
    B.   1
    C.   2
    D.   3
    E.   4

20. $\dfrac{2^{21}}{4^4\left(4^4 + 4^5\right)} =$

    A. $\dfrac{1}{4^4}$

    B. $\dfrac{1}{2^7}$

    C. $\dfrac{2^1}{2^5}$

    D. $\dfrac{2^5}{5}$

    E. $\dfrac{2^9}{17}$

21. What is the simplified expression of $\dfrac{x^{\frac{1}{3}} \times x^{\frac{3}{2}}}{x^{\frac{4}{3}} \times x^{\frac{3}{4}}}$?

    A. x^4

    B. $x^{\frac{-1}{2}}$

    C. x

    D. $x^{\frac{-1}{4}}$

    E. $x^{\frac{-4}{3}}$

Roots

A square root of a non-negative number x is a number that when multiplied by itself results in x. The square root is indicated by the radical sign ($\sqrt{\ }$). Roots beyond square, such as cube roots or fourth roots, are indicated by the appropriate number above the beginning of the radical sign, or by a fractional exponent.

Important Rules

$$\sqrt{a \times b} = \sqrt{a} \times \sqrt{b}$$

$$\sqrt{a} \times \sqrt{b} = \sqrt{a \times b}$$

$$a\sqrt{c} + b\sqrt{c} = (a + b)\sqrt{c}$$

$$\frac{\sqrt{a}}{\sqrt{b}} = \sqrt{\frac{a}{b}}$$

$$a^{\left(\frac{1}{b}\right)} = \sqrt[b]{a}$$

But:

$$\sqrt{a} + \sqrt{b} \neq \sqrt{a + b}$$

Example:

22. $\sqrt{75} + 3\sqrt{12} =$

    A. $11\sqrt{3}$
    B. $11\sqrt{6}$
    C. $17\sqrt{3}$
    D. $4\sqrt{87}$
    E. $30\sqrt{3}$

Practice Questions

23. What is a possible approximate value of x if $x^2 = 5.2 \times 10^{-7}$?

    A. 5.2×10^{-14}
    B. 2.5×10^{-7}
    C. 7.2×10^{-4}
    D. 2.5×10^{-2}
    E. -5.2×10^7

24. $\sqrt[3]{x^6 y^4 z^{-3}} =$

    A. $\dfrac{x^3 y^{\frac{3}{4}}}{z^{-1}}$

    B. $\dfrac{x^3 y^{\frac{4}{3}}}{z^1}$

    C. $\dfrac{x^2 y^{\frac{3}{4}}}{z^1}$

    D. $\dfrac{x^2 y^{\frac{4}{3}}}{z^1}$

    E. $\dfrac{x^2 y^{\frac{4}{3}}}{z^{-1}}$

25. The positive fourth root of x^3 times the positive square root of x equals 32. What is the value of x?

    A. 2
    B. 8
    C. 10
    D. 16
    E. 32

Equations

An equation is composed of two expressions on opposite sides of an equal sign where at least one of those expressions contains a variable representing an unknown value.

To solve an equation involving one or more variables, isolate the desired variable on one side of the equation.

The Golden Rule of Algebra requires you to perform the same operation on both sides of the equation. This includes addition, subtraction, multiplication, division, raising to an exponent or taking a root.

Example:

26. If $0.1m = 1$, what is the value of $1.1m$?

    A.   1.1
    B.   9.9
    C.   10
    D.   10.1
    E.   11

Practice Questions

27. What is the value of d if $\sqrt{(50 + 2d)} = 1 + d$?

    A. 6
    B. 7
    C. 8
    D. 9
    E. 10

28. $$\frac{2a + 3b + 2c}{3} = b$$

Quantity A	Quantity B
a	c

    A. Quantity A is greater.
    B. Quantity B is greater.
    C. The two quantities are equal.
    D. The relationship cannot be determined from the information given.

29. What is the value of s if 68% of $\frac{7}{s} = 5$?

    A. 0.485
    B. 0.867
    C. 0.952
    D. 1.05
    E. 2.05

Word Problems

Solving a Word Problem often involves translating a written scenario into mathematical terms.

Addition: *add, sum, total, net, together, gain*

Subtraction: *minus, difference, fewer, left, less, remaining, take away, remove, less than*

Multiplication: *multiple, product, at this rate, times, of*

Division: *divide, factor, per, each, quotient, ratio*

Example:

30. Which of the following equations can be used to find the value of y if 5 times the sum of y and 4 is 2 less than y?

    A. $y - 2 = 5(y + 4)$
    B. $y = 5(y + 4) - 2$
    C. $y - 2 = 5y + 4$
    D. $5(y + 2) = y + 4$
    E. $y = 5(y + 4 + 2)$

In addition, many Word Problems can be "mentally managed" by performing the following steps:

- Remove the word "if" or any synonyms such as "assuming" or "suppose".
- Wherever there is a comma, replace it with a period.
- Write down the given information on your scratch work and carefully label each item.

Example:

31. During the 19th century, a certain tribe collected 10 pieces of copper for every camel passing through Timbuktu in a caravan. If in 1880 an average of 8 caravans passed through Timbuktu every month, and there was an average of 100 camels in each caravan that year, how many pieces of copper did the tribe collect from caravans over the year?

    A. 800
    B. 8,000
    C. 9,600
    D. 80,000
    E. 96,000

    Scratch work:

Practice Questions

32. If Larry's weight were to decrease by 20 pounds, his new weight would be $\frac{7}{8}$ of his current weight. What is his current weight?

    A.   17.5 lb
    B.   22.9 lb
    C.   160 lb
    D.   180 lb
    E.   200 lb

33. A certain phone company charges $4.50 for the first 5 minutes of an international phone call. Additional time is charged at $0.50 per minute. How much would a customer be charged for an international phone call that started at 9:35 p.m. and ended at 11:15 p.m. the same day?

    A. $45.00
    B. $47.50
    C. $50.00
    D. $52.00
    E. $52.50

34. Greg drove 400 miles at a rate of 25 miles per hour. If during the same time, Andrew drove at 30 miles per hour, how many miles farther than Greg did Andrew drive?

    A.   16
    B.   80
    C.   330
    D.   400
    E.   480

Polynomials

Polynomials are algebraic expressions with more than one term (e.g., $x^2 + 2x$). The answers to polynomial equations often contain two possible values.

To multiply polynomials, use FOIL (multiply the First, then the Outer, then the Inner, then the Last terms).

Example:

35. $(x + 3)(x + 4) =$

    A. $x^2 + 7x + 12$
    B. $x^2 - 7x + 12$
    C. $x^2 + 7x - 12$
    D. $x^2 + x + 12$
    E. $x^2 - x - 12$

Reverse FOIL

To factor a polynomial, consider the signs of each term to establish positive and negative signs in each set of parentheses. Then factor the last term, looking for a pair of factors that add up to the middle term while taking positive and negative signs into account.

Example:

36. $x^2 + 5x - 6 =$

    A. $(x + 2)(x + 3)$
    B. $(x + 2)(x - 3)$
    C. $(x - 2)(x - 3)$
    D. $(x + 1)(x - 6)$
    E. $(x - 1)(x + 6)$

The most frequently tested polynomial problem solutions are:

$$a^2 + 2ab + b^2 = (a + b)^2$$
$$a^2 - 2ab + b^2 = (a - b)^2$$
$$a^2 - b^2 = (a - b)(a + b)$$

Practice Questions

37. If $n > 2$, which of the following expressions is equivalent to $\dfrac{3(n-2)+1}{(n+5)(n-2)}$?

   A. $\dfrac{3n-5}{n^2+3n-10}$

   B. $\dfrac{4}{n+5}$

   C. $3n - \dfrac{1}{n^2+3n-10}$

   D. $\dfrac{-5}{n^2-10}$

   E. $\dfrac{3n-3}{n^2+3n-3}$

38. What are the possible values of n if $n^2 + 7n - 5 = 3$?

   A. $\{-8, 1\}$
   B. $\{8, -1\}$
   C. $\{-3, 5\}$
   D. $\{2, -5\}$
   E. $\{-2, 5\}$

39. Factor $x^6 - 9y^4$ into the product of two binomial pairs.

   A. $(x^3 + 3y^2)(x^3 - 3y^2)$
   B. $(3x^3 + 3y^2)(3x^3 - 3y^2)$
   C. $(3x^3 + y^2)(3x^3 - y^2)$
   D. $(x^3 + 9y^2)(x^3 - 9y^2)$
   E. $(x^3 - 3y^2)(x^3 - 3y^2)$

Simultaneous Equations

Simultaneous equations include more than one variable.

There are two techniques for solving simultaneous equations.

Substitution

In this method, one equation is solved by isolating one variable. The resulting expression is substituted into the other equation to solve for the other variable. Substitution is useful when the value of one variable is already partially or fully solved for. In other words, at least one of the equations lacks one of the variables.

Combination (Elimination)

In this method, the equations are aligned such that a variable can be eliminated by subtraction. Combination is most useful in equations for which both variables need to be solved. In other words, all equations include all of the variables.

Example:

40. If $3a + 7b = 12$ and $a - b + 1 = 0$, what are the values of a and b?

    A. $a = \frac{1}{2}, b = \frac{3}{2}$

    B. $a = \frac{3}{2}, b = \frac{1}{2}$

    C. $a = -\frac{1}{11}, b = \frac{10}{11}$

    D. $a = \frac{10}{11}, b = -\frac{1}{11}$

    E. $a = 2, b = 3$

Substitution Solution:

Combination Solution:

Practice Questions

41. If $a = 3 + 3w$, $b = 5w - 7$, and $4a = 3b$, what does w equal?

    A.   10
    B.   11
    C.   12
    D.   13
    E.   15

42. A theater charges \$12 for seats in the orchestra and \$8 for seats in the balcony. On a certain night, a total of 350 tickets were sold, resulting in a total revenue of \$3,320. How many more tickets were sold that night for seats in the balcony than for seats in the orchestra?

    A.   90
    B.   110
    C.   120
    D.   130
    E.   220

43. If $p + 2q = 8$ and $2p - q = 11$, then $p = ?$

    A.   1

    B.   6

    C.   7

    D.   8

    E.   9

Absolute Values and Inequalities

Absolute Values

The absolute value sign indicates the distance a number is from zero on a number line.

When solving for a variable within the absolute value sign, separate the term within the absolute value sign into a positive and negative version and solve for both.

Example:

44. If $|x - 2| = 6$, which of the following sets represents all possible values of x?

    A. $\{8\}$
    B. $\{-4, 4\}$
    C. $\{-8, 8\}$
    D. $\{4, -8\}$
    E. $\{-4, 8\}$

Inequalities

To solve an inequality, perform the necessary operations to both sides of the inequality to isolate the variable.

If solving the inequality requires multiplying or dividing by a negative number, you must reverse the inequality sign.

When solving an inequality with an absolute value sign, solve both a positive and a negative version of the equation within the absolute value sign.

Example:

45.
$$1 < 3x + 5 < 17$$

    <u>Quantity A</u>   <u>Quantity B</u>
    The number of integer values for x 4

    A.   Quantity A is greater.
    B.   Quantity B is greater.
    C.   The two quantities are equal.
    D.   The relationship cannot be determined from the information given.

Practice Questions

46. If $|x + 4| > 1$, what are all possible values of x?

    A. $x > 3$ and $x < 5$

    B. $x > 3$ or $x < -5$

    C. $x > -3$ or $x < -5$

    D. $x > -3$ and $x < 5$

    E. $x > 3$

47. If $-6|4x + 2| = 96$, then x must

    A.   be greater than 2.

    B.   be an odd number.

    C.   be an even number.

    D.   not be a positive number.

    E.   not be a real number.

48. What are all the values of x for which $(x - 2)(x + 5) < 0$?

    A. $2 < x < 5$

    B. $-2 < x < 5$

    C. $-5 < x < 2$

    D. $x < -5$

    E. $x > 2$

Study Plan

After Class: Quantitative Reasoning 1

Complete Remaining *Lesson Book* Practice Questions   30m

Practice with Workshops

Data Sufficiency Basics Workshop   17m

Practice with Tests and Quizzes

Before Class: General Chemistry 1

Read *Review Notes* Chapters 22–27, 31–33   4h 30m

Quantum Number and Electron Configuration Workshop   45m

Reaction Types Workshop   45m

Chemical Kinetics Workshop   45m

Properties of Solutions Workshop   45m

Thermodynamics Workshop   45m

Skip Stoich Balancing (time suck)

GENERAL CHEMISTRY 1

TOPICS COVERED

- The General Chemistry Subsection
- Atomic and Molecular Structure
- Periodic Properties
- Stoichiometry
- Thermochemistry
- Equilibria
- Kinetics

After this session you will be able to:

- Differentiate between the different types of intramolecular and intermolecular bonds
- Predict properties based on those bonds and the periodic table
- Calculate stoichiometric values and balanced chemical equations
- Calculate energies based on thermodynamics
- Calculate properties of systems at equilibrium
- Determine chemical rate laws

The General Chemistry Subsection

Overview

- 30 questions (30% of the Survey of Natural Sciences section)

Topics

Atomic and Molecular Structure

- Electron Configuration
- Orbital Types
- Lewis-Dot Diagrams
- Atomic Theory
- Quantum Theory
- Molecular Geometry
- Bond Types
- Subatomic Particles

Periodic Properties

- Representative Elements
- Transition Elements
- Periodic Trends
- Descriptive Chemistry

Stoichiometry

- Percent Composition
- Empirical Formulas
- Balancing Equations
- Molecular Formulas
- Molar Mass
- Density
- Calculations from Equations

Chemical Equilibria

- Molecular
- Acids/Bases
- Precipitation
- Calculations
- Le Châtelier's Principle

Thermochemistry

- Laws of Thermodynamics
- Hess's Law
- Spontaneity
- Enthalpies and Entropies
- Heat Transfer

Chemical Kinetics

- Rate Laws
- Activation Energy
- Half-Life

Liquids and Solids

- Intermolecular Forces
- Phase Changes
- Vapor Pressure
- Structures
- Polarity
- Properties

Gases

- Kinetic Theory of Gases
- Dalton's Gas Law
- Boyle's Gas Law
- Charles's Gas Law
- Ideal Gas Law

Solutions

- Polarity
- Colligative Properties
- Forces
- Concentration Calculations

Acids and Bases

- pH
- Strength
- Brønsted-Lowry Reactions
- Calculations

Nuclear Reactions

- Balancing Equations
- Binding Energy
- Decay Processes
- Particles
- Terminology

Oxidation-Reduction Reactions

- Balancing Equations
- Oxidation Numbers
- Electrochemistry Calculations
- Electrochemistry Concepts

Laboratory

- Basic Techniques
- Equipment
- Error Analysis
- Safety
- Data Analysis

The Kaplan Question Strategy

STOP

→ Characterize the answer choices.

THINK

→ What is the question really asking?

→ What relevant information do you need?

PREDICT

→ Formulate a framework or prediction for your answer.

MATCH

→ Select the answer that truly meets the requirements of the prediction.

Atomic and Molecular Structure

Intramolecular Bonds

Ionic

Covalent

Metallic

Lewis-Dot Diagrams

Octet Rule

Formal Charge

Formal charge = valence e^- − number of π and σ bonds attached − nonbonding e^-

Resonance Structures

Practice Questions

1. Which of the following Lewis structures represents a compound free of formal charge that consists of one carbon atom, one hydrogen atom, one nitrogen atom, and one oxygen atom?

   I. $\ddot{O}=C=\ddot{N}-H$

   II. $:N\equiv C-\ddot{O}-H$

   III. $H-\ddot{O}=C=\ddot{N}$

   A.   I

   B.   II

   C.   I and II

   D.   II and III

   E.   I, II, and III

2. Possible structures of perchloric acid are shown below. Which is most stable?

A. 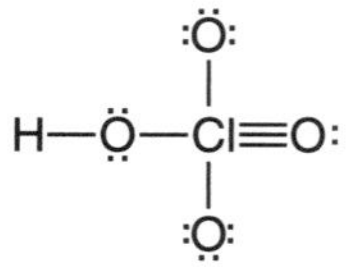 D.

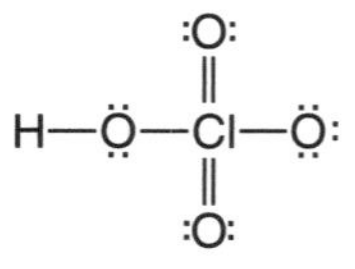

B. 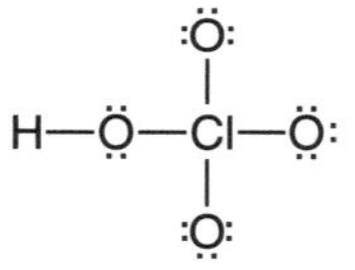 E.

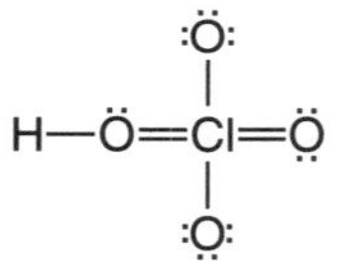

C.

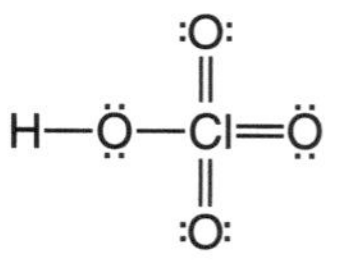

3. The correct order of decreasing individual bond strength between the nitrogen and oxygen atoms in the nitrate ion (NO_3^-), hydroxylamine (NH_2OH), the nitrosyl ion (NO^+), and the nitryl ion (NO_2^+) is

   A. $NO_3^- > NH_2OH > NO^+ > NO_2^+$

   B. $NO^+ > NO_2^+ > NO_3^- > NH_2OH$

   C. $NO^+ > NO_3^- > NO_2^+ > NH_2OH$

   D. $NH_2OH > NO_3^- > NO_2^+ > NO^+$

   E. $NO_3^- > NO^+ > NH_2OH > NO_2^+$

Molecular Geometry

Valence Shell Electron-Pair Repulsion Theory (VSEPR)

Bonding Pairs vs. Nonbonding Pairs

Electronic Geometry vs. Molecular Geometry

Electron pairs	Nonbonding pairs	Example	Geometric arrangement	Shape	Angles
2	0	$BeCl_2$	X — A — X	Linear	
3	0	BH_3		Trigonal planar	
4	0	CH_4		Tetrahedral	
4	1	NH_3		Trigonal pyramidal	
4	2	H_2O		Bent	
5	0	PCl_5		Trigonal bipyramidal	
6	0	SF_6		Octahedral	

Practice Questions

4. Which of the following molecules has the smallest bond angle?

    A. CH_4

    B. NH_3

    C. H_2O

    D. BH_3

    E. CO_2

5. Which of the following has a tetrahedral molecular geometry?

    A. ClO_3^-

    B. C_2H_4

    C. SO_4^{2-}

    D. H_2S

    E. NH_3

6. Which of the following does NOT have a tetrahedral electronic geometry?

    A. ClO_3^-

    B. C_2H_4

    C. SO_4^{2-}

    D. H_2S

    E. NH_3

Molecular Dipoles

Molecular dipoles depend on both individual bond dipoles and molecular geometry.

Intermolecular Forces

Intermolecular forces are a result of electrostatic interactions between charges or partial charges on different molecules.

Decreasing strength

1. _____

2. _____

3. _____

4. _____

5. _____

Practice Questions

7. Which of the following participate(s) in hydrogen bonding?

    A.   Methanol
    B.   Methane
    C.   Methanal
    D.   Bromomethane
    E.   All of the above

8. Which substance boils at the highest temperature?

    A.   Dimethyl ether (CH_3OCH_3)
    B.   Ethanol (CH_3CH_2OH)
    C.   Ethane (CH_3CH_3)
    D.   Chloroethane (CH_3CH_2Cl)
    E.   Ethanal (CH_3CHO)

9. Which represents the correct order of increasing boiling point?

    A.   water < acetone < methane < acetic acid
    B.   acetone < methane < acetic acid < water
    C.   methane < acetone < acetic acid < water
    D.   methane < acetone < water < acetic acid
    E.   acetone < water < methane < acetic acid

Quantum Numbers

Principal (n)

Angular (l)

Magnetic (m_l)

Spin (m_s)

Electron Configuration

Spectroscopic Notation

Hund's Rules

Aufbau Principle

STUDY TIP

Master the basics of General Chemistry first, starting with the level of the atom and building up to how different elements interact with one another. Progressing from small- to large-scale will help keep everything in perspective.

Practice Questions

10. What is the maximum number of electrons that can occupy a shell with a principal quantum number $n = 4$?

    A. 4
    B. 8
    C. 16
    D. 18
    E. 32

11. All of the following are possible principal and magnetic quantum numbers for an electron of a carbon atom in its ground state EXCEPT one. Which one is the EXCEPTION?

    A. $n = 1,$ $m_1 = 0$
    B. $n = 2,$ $m_1 = 0$
    C. $n = 2,$ $m_1 = -1$
    D. $n = 2,$ $m_1 = 1$
    E. $n = 3,$ $m_1 = -1$

12. Which of the following subshells will fill first?

    A. 5d
    B. 5f
    C. 6s
    D. 6p
    E. 4f

Periodic Properties

Isotope Notation

The Periodic Table

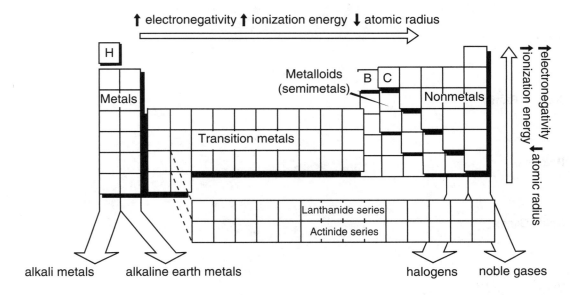

Representative Elements

Alkali Metals

Alkaline Earth Metals

Carbon Family

Nitrogen Family

Oxygen Family

Halogens

Noble Gases

Types of Elements

Metals

Nonmetals

Transition Metals

Metalloids

Periodic Trends

Effective Nuclear Charge (Z_{eff})

Atomic Radius

Electronegativity

Ionization Energy

Electron Affinity

TAKEAWAY

Knowing how the subatomic particles within an atom interact, especially in terms of Z_{eff}, makes understanding and memorizing all the periodic trends much easier.

Practice Questions

13. Isotopes always have the same

    A. atomic mass.
    B. mass number.
    C. atomic number.
    D. quantum number.
    E. molecular mass.

14. Among the transition metals essential to life, one finds V, Cr, Mn, Fe, Co, Ni, Cu, and Zn but not Sc or Ti. Which one of the following elements is also likely to be biologically important?

    A. Zr
    B. La
    C. Hf
    D. Mo
    E. Y

15. What is the electronic configuration of a free Fe^{3+} ion?

    A. $[Ar]3d^5$
    B. $[Ar]3d^6$
    C. $[Ar]3d^64s^2$
    D. $[Ar]4s^24p^3$
    E. $[Ar]4s^14d^4$

Practice Questions

16. Which of the following would be expected to have the largest atomic radius?

    A. Sn^{4-}
    B. Te^{2-}
    C. Te^{2+}
    D. Xe^{4+}
    E. Xe

17. Which of the following would require the greatest energy to remove an electron?

    A. K
    B. K^+
    C. K^-
    D. Na
    E. Na^+

18. The ionization energies below most likely correspond to which of the following elements?

First Ionization Energy	590 kJ/mol
Second Ionization Energy	1145 kJ/mol
Third Ionization Energy	4912 kJ/mol

    A. Na
    B. Ca
    C. N
    D. Ne
    E. P

Stoichiometry

Compound vs. Molecule

Molecular Mass vs. Molar Mass

Empirical vs. Molecular Formula

Percent Composition: percentage of mass contributed by each element in a compound

$$\% \text{ composition} = \frac{\text{Mass of X in formula}}{\text{Formula weight of compound}}$$

Practice Questions

19. What is the percent composition of chromium in $K_2Cr_2O_7$ (294.2 g•mol^{-1})?

    A.   18.2%
    B.   35.4%
    C.   44.4%
    D.   48.6%
    E.   52.0%

20. A compound with the empirical formula CH_2O has a weight of 180 g/mol. What is the molecular formula?

    A. CH_2O
    B. $C_2H_4O_2$
    C. $C_2H_6O_2$
    D. $C_6H_{12}O_6$
    E. $C_8H_{20}O_4$

21. What is the molecular formula of a compound composed of 40.9% carbon, 4.58% hydrogen, and 54.52% oxygen with a molecular weight of 264 g/mol?

    A. $C_9H_{12}O_9$
    B.   CHO
    C. CH_2O
    D. $C_3H_4O_3$
    E. $C_{10}H_{10}O$

Balancing Equations

$$\underline{} NaHCO_3 \rightarrow \underline{} Na_2CO_3 + \underline{} CO_2 + \underline{} H_2O$$

1. Write the unbalanced equation without coefficients.

2. Balance molecules containing the least represented element, found in the fewest number of reactants and products, first.

3. Balance remaining molecules, saving highly represented elements (often H and O) and elements by themselves (e.g., C (*s*)) for last.

4. If fractions are present, multiply every coefficient by the least common denominator so that all coefficients become whole numbers.

5. Check that the sums of elements and charges are equal on both sides of the equation.

Limiting Reactant

Stoichiometric Ratios

Theoretical Yield

Actual Yield

$$\text{Percent Yield} = \frac{\text{Actual Yield}}{\text{Theoretical Yield}} \times 100\%$$

TAKEAWAY

A calculator will not be available during the Survey of Natural Sciences section, so practice performing arithmetic mentally and by hand to quickly move through these types of calculations.

Practice Questions

22. When the following chemical reaction is balanced, what is the coefficient for O_2?

$$C_4H_{10} \ (l) + O_2 \ (g) \rightarrow CO_2 \ (g) + H_2O \ (l)$$

A. 1
B. 3
C. 8
D. 10
E. 13

23. According to the following equation, if there is 1 mol of A and 1 mol of B, which is the limiting reagent?

$$2\,A + B \rightarrow 2\,C + D$$

A. A
B. B
C. C
D. D
E. Both A and B

24. How many moles of B are needed to completely react with 1 mol of A given the following equation?

$$2\,A + 3\,B \rightarrow C$$

A. 1
B. 1.5
C. 2
D. 2.5
E. 3

25. How many grams of calcium chloride are needed to prepare 72.0 g of silver chloride according to the following equation?

$$CaCl_2 \ (aq) + 2\,AgNO_3 \ (aq) \rightarrow Ca(NO_3)_2 \ (aq) + 2\,AgCl \ (s)$$

A. 14.0 g
B. 27.9 g
C. 36.0 g
D. 55.8 g
E. 72.0 g

Thermochemistry

Enthalpy (ΔH)

Exothermic Reaction

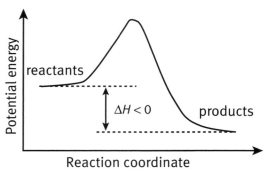

Endothermic Reaction

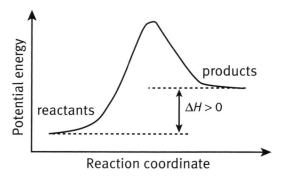

Transfer of Heat

$$\Delta U = Q - W_{\text{by system}}$$

Radiation

Conduction

Convection

Bond Energy

Standard Heat of Formation (ΔH_f°)

$$\Delta H_{\text{rxn}}^{\circ} = (\text{sum of } \Delta H_{\text{products}}^{\circ}) - (\text{sum of } \Delta H_{\text{reactants}}^{\circ})$$

Hess's Law

If a reaction can be broken down into a series of steps, the enthalpy change for the overall net reaction is the sum of the enthalpies of each step.

Practice Questions

26. Given the thermochemical equations below, calculate ΔH_{rxn}° for the reaction.

$$3\,C\,(s) + 4\,H_2\,(g) \rightarrow C_3H_8\,(g)$$

a) $C_3H_8\,(g) + 5\,O_2\,(g) \rightarrow 3\,CO_2\,(g) + 4\,H_2O\,(l)$ $\Delta H_a^{\circ} = -2220.1$ kJ

b) $C\,(s) + O_2\,(g) \rightarrow CO_2\,(g)$ $\Delta H_b^{\circ} = -393.5$ kJ

c) $H_2\,(g) + \frac{1}{2}\,O_2\,(g) \rightarrow H_2O\,(l)$ $\Delta H_c^{\circ} = -285.8$ kJ

  A.   −4544 kJ/mol
  B.   −2872 kJ/mol
  C.   −103.6 kJ/mol
  D.   467.9 kJ/mol
  E.   1541 kJ/mol

27. The bond energy of the N−H bond is 389 kJ/mol, the bond energy of the O=O bond is 498, and the bond enthalpy of the N≡N bond is 941 kJ/mol. Given the following chemical reaction, what is the bond energy of the O−H bond?

$$4\,NH_3 + 3\,O_2 \rightarrow 2\,N_2 + 6\,H_2O \qquad\qquad \Delta H_{rxn}^{\circ} = -1266$ kJ$$

  A.   71 kJ/mol
  B.   251 kJ/mol
  C.   324 kJ/mol
  D.   462 kJ/mol
  E.   1033 kJ/mol

28. Consider the following reaction:

$$C_2H_2 + \frac{5}{2}\,O_2 \rightarrow 2\,CO_2 + H_2O \qquad\qquad \Delta H_{rxn}^{\circ} = -1255.5$ kJ/mol$$

If the ΔH_f° of CO_2 is −393.5 kJ/mol and the ΔH_f° of H_2O is −241.8 kJ/mol, what is the ΔH_f° of acetylene, C_2H_2?

  A.   −620.1 kJ/mol
  B.   −226.6 kJ/mol
  C.   0 kJ/mol
  D.   226.6 kJ/mol
  E.   620.1 kJ/mol

Entropy (ΔS)

Gibbs Free Energy (ΔG)

$\Delta G = \Delta H - T\Delta S$

$\Delta G < 0$: _____

$\Delta G = 0$: _____

$\Delta G > 0$: _____

STUDY TIP

Be careful with the minus signs! Focus on whether energy is leaving or being added rather than attempting to follow the thermochemistry equations strictly.

Practice Questions

29. Which of the following occurs when frozen ice melts into liquid water?

    A.   The enthalpy increases, and the entropy increases.
    B.   The enthalpy decreases, and the entropy increases.
    C.   The enthalpy increases, and the entropy decreases.
    D.   The enthalpy decreases, and the entropy decreases.
    E.   The enthalpy increases, and the entropy remains the same.

30. Which of the following defines a reaction that is temperature-dependent?

    I.   Positive ΔH, positive ΔS
    II.   Positive ΔH, negative ΔS
    III.   Negative ΔH, positive ΔS
    IV.   Negative ΔH, negative ΔS

    A.   I and II
    B.   I and III
    C.   I and IV
    D.   II and III
    E.   III and IV

31. While standing in the ocean, you begin to feel cold. This is because heat is transferring from you to the water, which mainly occurs through the process of

    A.   radiation.
    B.   conduction.
    C.   convection.
    D.   advection.
    E.   changing phase.

Equilibria

Molecular Equilibrium

Reaction Quotient (Q)

For a reaction $aA + bB \rightleftharpoons cC + dD$,

$$Q = \frac{[\text{products}]}{[\text{reactants}]} = \frac{[C]^c [D]^d}{[A]^a [B]^b}$$

Equilibrium Constant (K_{eq})

$K_{eq} > Q$: _____

$K_{eq} = Q$: _____

$K_{eq} < Q$: _____

Le Châtelier's Principle

If a stress (a change in concentration, pressure, or temperature) is applied to a system at equilibrium, the system will shift in such a way as to relieve the applied stress.

Solution Equilibrium

Ion Product (Q_{sp})

Solubility Product Constant (K_{sp})

$K_{sp} > Q_{sp}$: _____

$K_{sp} = Q_{sp}$: _____

$K_{sp} < Q_{sp}$: _____

Molar Solubility

Common Ion Effect

Kaplan Method for Equilibrium Questions

1. Write down a balanced reaction (if not given).

2. Find the expression for the K_{value}.

3. Plug into the K expression.

TEST DAY TIP
Questions regarding Stoichiometry, Balancing Equations, and Equilibrium can be very time-consuming on Test Day, so triage them for later if they will involve heavy calculations.

Practice Questions

System 1

$$2 \text{ PbSO}_4 \, (s) + 2 \text{ H}_2\text{O} \, (l) \leftrightharpoons \text{Pb} \, (s) + \text{PbO}_2 \, (s) + 2 \text{ HSO}_4^- \, (aq) + 2 \text{ H}^+ \, (aq)$$

32. What effect would increasing the amount of Pb (s) have on System 1?

    A.   The reaction would proceed in reverse to form more of both reactants.
    B.   The reaction would proceed in reverse to produce more PbSO_4 only.
    C.   The reaction would proceed forward to form more of all the products.
    D.   The reaction would proceed forward to produce more H^+ only.
    E.   There would be no net effect.

33. What would happen if the pH of System 1 were increased?

    A.   The reaction would proceed in reverse to form more of both reactants.
    B.   The reaction would proceed in reverse to produce more PbSO_4 only.
    C.   The reaction would proceed forward to form more of all the products.
    D.   The reaction would proceed forward to produce more H^+ only.
    E.   There would be no net effect.

34. What would happen to System 1 if the pressure were increased?

    A.   The reaction would proceed in reverse to form more of both reactants.
    B.   The reaction would proceed in reverse to produce more PbSO_4 only.
    C.   The reaction would proceed forward to form more of all the products.
    D.   The reaction would proceed forward to produce more H^+ only.
    E.   There would be no net effect.

Practice Questions

35. The solubility of FeF_2 in an aqueous solution was determined to be 1.9×10^{-2} mol/L. What is the value of the K_{sp} for FeF_2?

    A. 3.3×10^{-10}
    B. 6.8×10^{-6}
    C. 2.7×10^{-5}
    D. 1.4×10^{-3}
    E. 1.4×10^{-1}

36. What is the molar solubility of silver chloride solution in a 0.1 M solution of table salt ($K_{sp} = 1.6 \times 10^{-10}$)?

    A. 2.6×10^{-20}
    B. 1.6×10^{-9}
    C. 4.0×10^{-5}
    D. 1.6×10^{-5}
    E. 4.0×10^{-4}

37. If 1.0 mL of a 1.0×10^{-5} M NaSCN solution is added to 3.0 mL of a 1.0×10^{-5} M $AgNO_3$ solution, will there be any precipitate? (K_{sp} of AgSCN $= 1.0 \times 10^{-12}$)

    A.   No, both NaSCN and $AgNO_3$ are completely soluble.
    B.   No, all ion concentrations are at or below saturation levels.
    C.   No, NaSCN is hygroscopic, so it will undergo a side reaction with water.
    D.   Yes, both AgSN and $NaNO_3$ are completely insoluble.
    E.   Yes, Ag^+ and SCN^- concentrations are above saturation levels.

Kinetics

Rate Laws

For a reaction $aA + bB \rightleftharpoons cC + dD$,

$Rate = k\,[A]^X\,[B]^Y$

k = rate constant

$X + Y$ = order of reaction

Reaction Orders

Zero order

First order

Second order

Determining Orders

Trial	$[A]_{initial}$ (M)	$[B]_{initial}$ (M)	$r_{initial}$ (M/sec)
1	1.0	1.0	2.0
2	1.0	2.0	8.1
3	2.0	2.0	15.9

Factors Affecting Rate

Reaction Concentration

Temperature

Medium

Catalyst

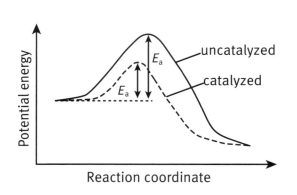

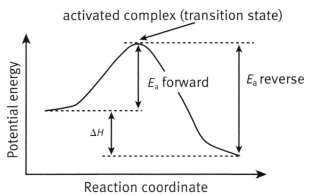

Practice Questions

38. Given the experimental data below, determine the rate law for the following reaction.

$$2\,H_2O_2\,(aq) + I^-\,(aq) \rightarrow O_2\,(g) + 2\,H_2O\,(l) + I^-\,(aq)$$

Trial	$[KI]_{initial}$ (M)	$[H_2O_2]_{initial}$ (M)	Rate of O_2 formation (mol $\cdot$ L^{-1} $\cdot$ s^{-1})
1	0.060	0.040	3.61×10^{-8}
2	0.060	0.080	7.25×10^{-8}
3	0.090	0.040	5.39×10^{-8}

- A. Rate $= k[H_2O_2]$
- B. Rate $= k[I^-][H_2O_2]$
- C. Rate $= k[I^-][H_2O_2]^2$
- D. Rate $= k[I^-]^2[H_2O_2]$
- E. Rate $= k[I^-]^2[H_2O_2]^2$

39. If the rate law of the reaction that follows the mechanism below is determined to be $k[H^+][I^-][H_2O_2]$, then what is the rate-limiting step?

$H_2O_2 + H^+ \rightleftharpoons H_3O_2^+$	Step 1
$I^- + H_3O_2^+ \rightarrow HOI + H_2O$	Step 2
$I^- + HOI \rightarrow I_2 + OH^-$	Step 3
$H^+ + OH^- \rightarrow H_2O$	Step 4

- A. Step 1
- B. Step 2
- C. Step 3
- D. Step 4
- E. Cannot be determined

40. Which of the following is least likely to increase the rate of a reaction not at equilibrium?

- A. Increasing the temperature
- B. Adding more reactant
- C. Removing product
- D. Adding a catalyst
- E. Adding an enzyme

Study Plan

After Class: General Chemistry 1

Complete Remaining *Lesson Book* Practice Questions	30m	
Practice with Tests and Quizzes		

Before Class: Organic Chemistry 1

Read *Review Notes* Chapters 38–43	3h 0m	
Nomenclature and Functional Groups Workshop	45m	

ORGANIC CHEMISTRY 1

TOPICS COVERED

- The Organic Chemistry Subsection
- Nomenclature
- Stereochemistry
- Mechanisms

After this session you will be able to:

- Assign names to molecules
- Differentiate among different types of isomers
- Identify types of substitution, elimination, and addition reactions
- Describe the properties of those reactions

The Organic Chemistry Subsection

Overview

- 30 questions (30% of the Survey of the Natural Sciences section)

Topics

Mechanisms: Energetics, Structure, and Stability of Intermediates

- Elimination
- Addition
- Free Radical
- Substitution

Chemical and Physical Properties of Molecules and Organic Analysis

- Intermolecular Forces
  1. Solubility
  2. Melting/Boiling Points
- Laboratory Theory and Techniques
  1. TLC
  2. Separation
- Spectroscopy
  1. ^{1}H NMR
  2. ^{13}C NMR
  3. Infrared
  4. Multi-spectra
- Polarity

Stereochemistry

- Chirality
- Isomer Relationships
- Conformations

Nomenclature

- IUPAC Rules
- Functional Groups in Molecules

Reactions of the Major Functional Groups

- Alkene/Alkyne
- Aromatic
- Substitution/Elimination
- Aldehyde/Ketone
- Carboxylic Acids and Derivatives

Acid-Base Chemistry

- Ranking Acidity/Basicity
  1. Structure Analysis
  2. pH/pK_a Data Analysis
- Prediction of Products and Equilibria

Aromatics and Bonding

- Aromaticity
- Resonance
- Atomic/Molecular Orbitals
- Hybridization
- Bond Angles/Lengths

The Kaplan Question Strategy

STOP

➜ Characterize the answer choices.

THINK

➜ What is the question really asking?

➜ What relevant information do you need?

PREDICT

➜ Formulate a framework or prediction for your answer.

MATCH

➜ Select the answer that truly meets the requirements of the prediction.

Nomenclature

IUPAC Rules

1. Identify the longest carbon chain containing the highest-priority functional group.
2. Number the carbon chain so the highest-priority functional group receives the lowest number and becomes the suffix.
3. Number the remaining substituents accordingly, including them as prefixes in alphabetical order.

Carbon Chains

Carbons	Prefix
1	Meth–
2	Eth–
3	Prop–
4	But–
5	Pent–
6	Hex–
7	Hept–
8	Oct–
9	Non–
10	Dec–

Functional Groups

Functional Group	Structure	IUPAC
Alkane	H H | | —C—C— | | H H	–ane
Alkene	H H | | —C=C—	–ene
Alkyne	—C≡C—	–yne
Phenyl	H H \ / C=C / \ H—C C— \ / C—C / \ H H	phenyl–
Alkyl Halide	X | —C— | (X = F, Cl, Br, I)	halo– and –halide
Acyl Halide	O || — C —X	halocarbonyl– and –oyl halide
Alcohol	OH | —C— |	hydroxy– and –ol
Aldehyde	O || —C—H	oxo– and –al
Ketone	O || —C—	oxo– and –one
Carboxylic Acid	O || —C—OH	carboxy– and –oic acid
Ether	| | —C—O—C— | |	alkoxy– and –ether
Ester	O || | —C—O—C— |	alkoxycarbonyl– and –oate

Functional Group	Structure	IUPAC
Amine	$\begin{array}{c} NH_2 \\ | \\ -C- \\ | \end{array}$	amino– and –amine
Amide	$\begin{array}{c} O \\ || \\ -C-NH_2 \end{array}$	amido– and –amide
Imine	$\begin{array}{c} | \\ -C=N- \end{array}$	imino– and –imine
Nitrile	$-C\equiv N$	cyano– and –nitrile
Thiol	$\begin{array}{c} SH \\ | \\ -C- \\ | \end{array}$	sulfhydryl– and –thiol

TAKEAWAY

Even though Nomenclature by itself is only worth three points on Test Day, you will need to rely on your knowledge of IUPAC rules and functional groups to be able to answer many of the other questions in the Organic Chemistry section.

Practice Questions

1. Compound E reacts with semicarbazide to form the semicarbazone F according to the following equation:

Compound F contains what functional groups?

A. Imine, amine, amide
B. Imine, amine, carbonyl
C. Amine, amide, hydroxyl
D. Phenyl, amide, imine
E. Ethyl, amide, ketone

2. What is the correct IUPAC name for the compound below?

A. 1-phenylethanol
B. 2-ethylphenol
C. 2-phenylethanol
D. Methyl phenyl ketone
E. 1-hydroxymethylphenyl

3. Name the organic reactant and product of the following reaction.

A. 3-propylpentanol, 3-ethyl-2-pentene
B. 2-ethylbutanol, 3-ethyl-3-pentene
C. t-butylpentanol, isoheptene
D. 3-ethyl-3-pentanol, 3-ethyl-2-pentene
E. 3-ethyl-3-pentanol, isopentene

Stereochemistry

Conformational Isomers

Newman Projections

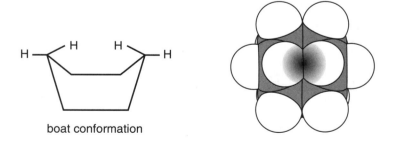

Torsional Strain

staggered (*anti*)	staggered (*gauche*)	totally eclipsed	eclipsed

Cycloalkanes

boat conformation

Substituted Cycloalkanes

Ring Strain

Practice Questions

4. Which of the following conformations of 1-*t*-butyl-2,4-dichlorocyclohexane is the least stable?

A.

D.

B.

E.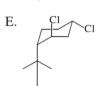

C.

5. Which of the following conformations is the most stable?

A.

D. CH₃ CH₃

B. CH₃ CH₃

E. CH₃ CH₃

C. CH₃ H₃C

6. Which of the following correctly ranks the cycloalkanes in decreasing order of ring strain?

    A.   Cyclobutane > cyclopentane > cyclohexane > cyclopropane
    B.   Cyclohexane > cyclobutane > cyclopentane > cyclopropane
    C.   Cyclopentane > cyclopropane > cyclobutane > cyclohexane
    D.   Cyclohexane > cyclopropane > cyclobutane > cyclopentane
    E.   Cyclopropane > cyclobutane > cyclopentane > cyclohexane

Enantiomers

Fischer Projections

$$H \overset{\displaystyle Br}{\underset{\displaystyle CH_2OH}{\rule[0.5em]{2em}{0.4pt}}} CHO \quad \equiv \quad H \overset{\displaystyle Br}{\underset{\displaystyle CH_2OH}{\rule[0.5em]{2em}{0.4pt}}} CHO$$

Chirality

Designating the Molecule as *R* or *S*

1. Put the atoms attached directly to the chiral center in descending order by molecular weight of the attached atom.

2. Ignore priority 4 and draw an arrow connecting $1 \to 2 \to 3$.

3. Note the direction of the arrow as clockwise (*R*) or counterclockwise (*S*).

4. If priority 4 is going into the page (going away), keep the designation as it is.
   If priority 4 is coming out of the page (coming forward), switch the designation (e.g., *R* to *S*).

Optical Activity

Racemic Mixture

Diastereomers

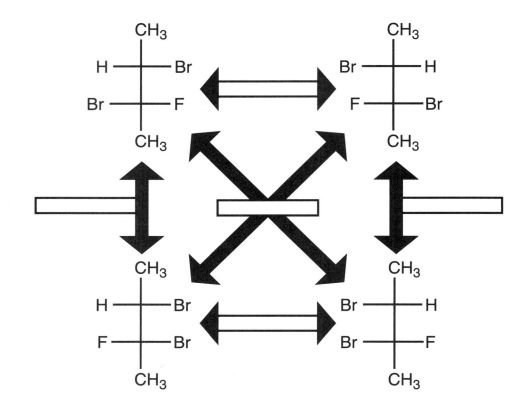

Meso Compounds

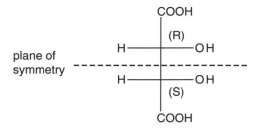

Practice Questions

7. Cholesterol, shown below, contains how many chiral centers?

H_3C ,,,, $-(CH_2)_3C(CH_3)_2H$

A. 5
B. 7
C. 8
D. 9
E. 11

8. Which of the following compounds is optically inactive?

A.
CH_3
H——Cl
Cl——H
CH_3

C.
CH_3
H——Cl
H——Cl
CH_3

E.
CH_2Cl
H——Cl
H——Cl
CH_3

B.
CH_3
Cl——H
H——Cl
CH_3

D.
CH_2Cl
H——Cl
H——H
CH_3

9. How many chiral centers does thyroid hormone (shown below) have, and how should the chiral center(s) be designated?

A. 1 chiral center; *R* configuration
B. 1 chiral center; *S* configuration
C. 2 chiral centers; both *R* configuration
D. 2 chiral centers; both *S* configuration
E. 2 chiral centers; one *R* configuration, one *S* configuration

Cis-Trans Isomers

H3CH2C   CH3
   \   /
    C = C
   /   \
  H   H

_____

H3CH2C   H
   \   /
    C = C
   /   \
  H   CH3

_____

E-Z Isomers

H3C   H
   \   /
    C = C
   /   \
  Cl   CH2CH3

_____

H3C   CH2CH3
   \   /
    C = C
   /   \
  Cl   H

_____

Practice Questions

10. Which molecule has the lowest boiling point?

   A. *cis*-2-Butene
   B. *trans*-2-Butene
   C. *cis*-3-Hexene
   D. *trans*-3-Hexene
   E. *cis*-4-Octene

11. Which term best describes the following molecules?

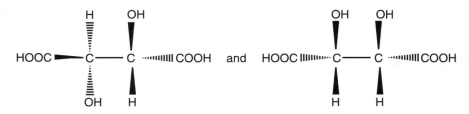

   A. Conformational isomers
   B. Identical compounds
   C. Enantiomers
   D. Geometric isomers
   E. Meso compounds

12. Which term best describes the following molecules?

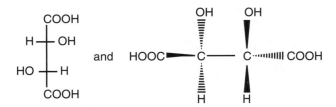

   A. Conformational isomers
   B. Identical compounds
   C. Enantiomers
   D. Geometric isomers
   E. Meso compounds

Mechanisms

Nucleophiles

Electrophiles

Leaving Groups

Substitution: S$_N$1

Alkyl halide — slow — Carbocation intermediate + X$^\ominus$ — Substituted product

: Nu$^\ominus$

Mechanism

Kinetics

Substrate

Nucleophiles

Leaving Groups

Solvents

Stereochemistry

Example

Practice Questions

13. Which of the following is the best leaving group?

    A. F^-
    B. Cl^-
    C. Br^-
    D. I^-
    E. H^-

14. Each of the following statements correctly describes an S_N1 reaction EXCEPT one. Which one is the EXCEPTION?

    A.   The reaction follows first-order kinetics.
    B.   The intermediate is a carbocation.
    C.   The carbocation stability follows the trend $3° > 2° > 1°$.
    D.   Polar aprotic solvents stabilize the carbocation by hydrogen bonding.
    E.   If the substrate is optically active, a racemic mixture results.

15. A chemist wants to increase the rate of an S_N1 reaction. Which of the following strategies would be most effective?

    A.   Reacting the substrate with a stronger nucleophile.
    B.   Performing the reaction in an aprotic solvent.
    C.   Selecting a substrate that will form a primary carbocation.
    D.   Using a substrate with a better leaving group.
    E.   Replacing the weak nucleophile with an equal concentration of strong base.

Substitution: S$_N$2

Alkyl halide   Transition state   Substituted product

(R = alkyl group or — H)

Mechanism

Kinetics

Substrates

Nucleophiles

Leaving Groups

Solvents

Stereochemistry

$$CH_3CO_2^- + \quad \underset{R'}{\overset{H}{\underset{\text{R''}}{C}}}-I \longrightarrow CH_3CO_2-\underset{R'}{\overset{H}{\underset{\text{R''}}{C}}} + I^-$$

Example

Transition state

Practice Questions

16. How would the reaction profile for an S_N2 reaction be different if using a secondary substrate instead of a primary substrate?

   A. The reaction with a secondary substrate would have a significantly higher activation energy.

   B. The reaction with a secondary substrate would have a significantly lower activation energy.

   C. The reaction with a secondary substrate would have a significantly higher energy of products.

   D. The reaction with a secondary substrate would have a significantly lower energy of reactants.

   E. The reaction with a secondary substrate would follow second-order kinetics, while the reaction with the primary substrate would follow first-order kinetics.

17. The rate law for an S_N2 reaction is best described as

   A. rate = k[nucleophile].

   B. rate = k[alkyl halide].

   C. rate = k[alkyl halide]^2.

   D. rate = k[alkyl halide][nucleophile].

   E. rate = k[alkyl halide][nucleophile]^2.

18. Which of the following alkyl halides will be the most suitable for an S_N2 reaction?

   A. CH_3Cl

   B.

   C.

   D.

   E.

Elimination: E1

Base **:**

	slow		

Alkyl halide

Carbocation
intermediate

Elimination product

+ HX

Mechanism

Kinetics

Substrates

Bases

Leaving Groups

Solvents

Stereochemistry

Competition

Example

Elimination: E2

Alkyl halide   Elimination product

Mechanism

Kinetics

Substrates

Bases

Leaving Groups

Solvents

Stereochemistry

anti-periplanar
(staggered)

Competition

Example

Practice Questions

19. Which of the following is the best solvent for an E2 reaction?

    A. Water
    B. Alcohol
    C. Acetone
    D. Hexane
    E. Ammonia

20. The rate-determining (slow) step in an E1 reaction is the

    A. nucleophilic attack on the substrate.
    B. formation of the carbocation intermediate.
    C. formation of the chiral transition state.
    D. inversion of configuration of the alkyl halide.
    E. formation of the double bond.

21. The dehydration of 2-methylcyclohexanol is an illustration of Zaitsev's rule, which states: In a β-elimination reaction, the most highly substituted alkene will be the major product. Assuming the following reaction follows an E2 mechanism, predict the product distribution.

    A. Only product 1 will be formed.
    B. Only product 2 will be formed.
    C. Product 1 will be the major product, and product 2 will be the minor product.
    D. Product 2 will be the major product, and product 1 will be the minor product.
    E. Both Products 1 and 2 will be formed in equal amounts.

Substitution and Elimination Reactions Overview

When predicting the reactivity of a substrate with respect to S_N2, S_N1, E2, and E1 reactions, ask the following questions:

1. Would the carbocation be stable if the leaving group dissociated?

    If no, rule out S_N1 and E1.

2. Is there a good nucleophile?

    If no, rule out S_N2.

3. Is there a strong base available to attack the substrate?

    If no, rule out E2.

4. Does the nucleophile have easy access to the side of the substrate opposite the leaving group?

    If no, rule out S_N2.

Reactivity in Aprotic Solvent

Substrate	Good Nu., Weak Base (e.g., Cl^-)	Good Nu., Strong Base (e.g., OH^-)	Bulky Nu., Strong Base (e.g., *t*-butoxide)
Methyl			
1°			
2°			
3°			

Practice Questions

22. What is the major product of the following reaction?

$$(CH_3)_2CHCHOHCH_2CH_3 \xrightarrow[\text{Heat}]{H_2SO_4}$$

A.

B.

C.

D.

E.

23. A chemist wants to ensure that the chemical reaction he is about to perform will follow the S_N2 mechanism. How can he promote S_N2 over E2?

   A.   He can use a substrate with a bulkier base.
   B.   He can add heat to the reaction.
   C.   He can use a good leaving group.
   D.   He can use a substrate with tertiary substitution.
   E.   He can use a good nucleophile that is not a strong base.

24. (R)-1-fluoro-1-iodopropane is reacted with NaN_3 in HMPA. Which of the following is the major product of this reaction?

   A.   (R)-1-azido-1-fluoropropane
   B.   (R)-1-azido-1-iodopropane
   C.   (S)-1-azido-fluoropropane
   D.   (S)-1-azido-fluoropropene
   E.   A racemic mixture of (R)-1-azido-1-fluoropropane and (S)-1-azido-1-fluoropropane

Substitution: Radical

General Reactions

Initiation: $\qquad X_2 \xrightarrow[\text{or } \Delta]{hv} 2\,X\bullet$

Propagation: $\qquad X\bullet + RH \rightarrow HX + R\bullet$

$\qquad\qquad\quad R\bullet + X_2 \rightarrow RX + X\bullet$

Termination: $\qquad 2\,X\bullet \rightarrow X_2$

$\qquad\qquad\quad X\bullet + R\bullet \rightarrow RX$

$\qquad\qquad\quad 2\,R\bullet \rightarrow R_2$

Practice Questions

25. Which of the following is the most likely intermediate for the following reaction?

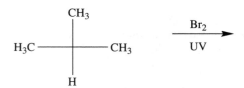

A. $H_3C \overset{\bullet}{\underset{\underset{H_3C}{|}}{C}} CH_3$

D. $H_3C \overset{-}{\underset{\underset{CH_3}{|}}{C}} CH_3$

B. $H_3C \underset{\underset{CH_3}{|}}{\overset{\overset{H}{|}}{C}} \overset{\bullet}{CH_2}$

E. $\overset{\bullet}{H_2C} \underset{\underset{CH_3}{|}}{\overset{\overset{H}{|}}{C}} \overset{\bullet}{CH_2}$

C. $H_3C \underset{\underset{CH_3}{|}}{\overset{+}{C}} CH_3$ (with CH₃ groups)

26. Which of the following is a chain-termination step?

A. $Cl\bullet + Cl\bullet \rightarrow Cl_2$
B. $Cl\bullet + CH_4 \rightarrow CH_3CH_3HCl$
C. $CH_3\bullet + Cl_2 \rightarrow CH_3Cl + Cl\bullet$
D. $CH_3\bullet + Cl\bullet \rightarrow CH_3Cl_2Cl + Cl\bullet$
E. $Cl_2 \rightarrow 2\ Cl\bullet$

27. What alkyl halide will be the major product from the reaction of excess butane with I_2 in the presence of light?

A. 1-Iodobutane
B. 2-Iodobutane
C. 1,2-Diiodobutane
D. Iodoethane
E. No reaction will occur.

Addition

Markovnikov Addition

Alkene + Hydrogen Halide → Halogen on more-substituted carbon of alkane

Anti-Markovnikov Addition

Alkene + Halogen Radical → Halogen on less-substituted carbon of alkane

Anti Addition of Halogens

Alkene + X_2 → Halogenated Alkane

Dibromination to Synthesize Alkynes from Alkenes

$$RHC = CHR + Br_2 \xrightarrow{\text{(addition rxn)}} R-\overset{\overset{\displaystyle H}{|}}{\underset{\underset{\displaystyle Br}{|}}{C}}-\overset{\overset{\displaystyle Br}{|}}{\underset{\underset{\displaystyle H}{|}}{C}}-R$$

vic-dibromide

$$R-\overset{\overset{\displaystyle H}{|}}{\underset{\underset{\displaystyle Br}{|}}{C}}-\overset{\overset{\displaystyle Br}{|}}{\underset{\underset{\displaystyle H}{|}}{C}}-R + NH_2^- \longrightarrow R-\overset{\overset{\displaystyle H}{|}}{C}=\overset{}{\underset{\underset{\displaystyle Br}{|}}{C}}-R + NH_3 + Br^-$$

$$R-\overset{\overset{\displaystyle H}{|}}{C}=\overset{}{\underset{\underset{\displaystyle Br}{|}}{C}}-R + NH_2^- \longrightarrow R-C \equiv C-R + NH_3 + Br^-$$

STUDY TIP

Rather than trying to memorize each individual mechanism, learn the similarities and differences between substitution, elimination, and addition reactions. This will allow you to more easily understand the material and help you answer a variety of questions on Test Day.

Practice Questions

28. What is the product of the following reaction?

$$CH_3CH_2CH=CH_2 + HBr \longrightarrow$$

A. 1-Bromobutane
B. 2-Bromobutane
C. 1,2-Dibromobutane
D. 1-Bromopropane
E. No reaction will occur.

29. What is the product of the following reaction?

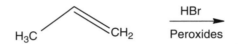

A. 1-Bromopropane
B. 2-Bromopropane
C. 1,2-Dibromopropane
D. 1-Bromopropene
E. No reaction will occur.

30. 2-Methyl-2-butene was reacted to form a tertiary alkyl halide. Which reagent is most likely to have caused this reaction?

A. HF with light
B. CH_3OOCH_3 alone
C. HI with heat
D. HCl with light
E. HBr alone

Study Plan

After Class: Organic Chemistry 1

Complete Remaining *Lesson Book* Practice Questions   30m

Practice with Tests and Quizzes

Practice Tests

Full-Length Test 1   4h 30m

Before Class: Biology 2

Read *Review Notes* Chapters 10–18   4h 30m

BIOLOGY 2

TOPICS COVERED

- Anatomy and Physiology
- Cell and Molecular Biology
- Developmental Biology

After this session you will be able to:

- Recall the structures and functions of the digestive, circulatory, respiratory, musculoskeletal, nervous, endocrine, urinary, integumentary, immunological, and reproductive systems
- Describe the steps of mitosis and meiosis
- Describe the stages of embryonic development

Anatomy and Physiology

Digestive System

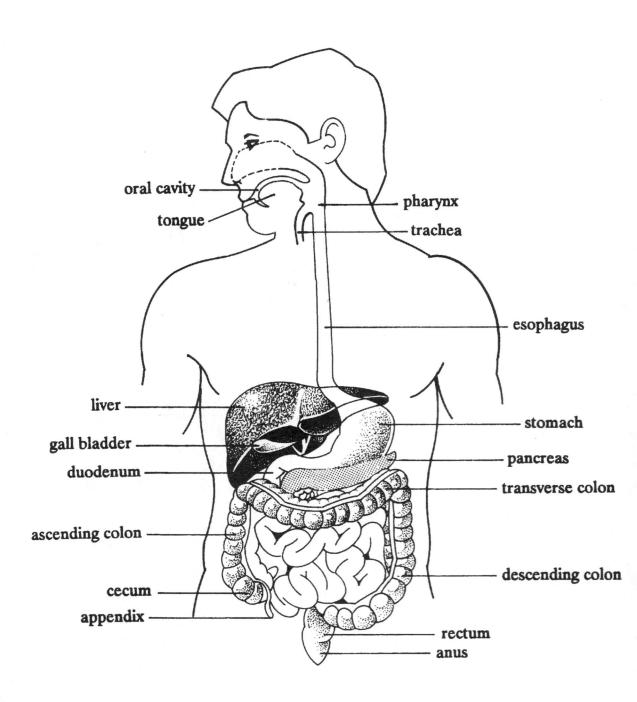

oral cavity

tongue

pharynx

trachea

esophagus

liver

stomach

gall bladder

pancreas

duodenum

transverse colon

ascending colon

descending colon

cecum

appendix

rectum

anus

Components of the Digestive Tract

Mouth

Esophagus

Stomach

Small Intestine

Large Intestine

Liver

Gall Bladder

Pancreas

Practice Questions

1. A certain individual lacks the enzyme maltase, which breaks down the disaccharide maltose into glucose monosaccharides. Which of the following is most likely to occur?

   A.   Maltose will be digested by the lactase enzymes in the small intestine.
   B.   Maltose will not be absorbed by active transport but will passively diffuse into the cells of the intestinal epithelium.
   C.   Maltose will be anaerobically digested by the bacteria in the gut.
   D.   Maltose will be flagged as a foreign body and attacked by the immune system.
   E.   The individual will be susceptible to malnutrition due to an inability to absorb glucose.

2. Which biological molecules does salivary amylase break down?

   A.   Proteins
   B.   Lipids
   C.   Monosaccharides
   D.   Nucleic acids
   E.   Starches

3. Which of the following best describes the role of bacteria in the human large intestine?

   A.   Prevent invasion of opportunistic species
   B.   Ferment undigested carbohydrates
   C.   Produce vitamin K
   D.   Create methane gas as a byproduct of metabolism
   E.   All of the above

Circulatory System

Blood Components

Erythrocytes

Leukocytes

Thrombocytes

Plasma

Blood Types

Blood type	Antigens	Antibodies	Receives from	Donates to
AB⁺				
O⁻				

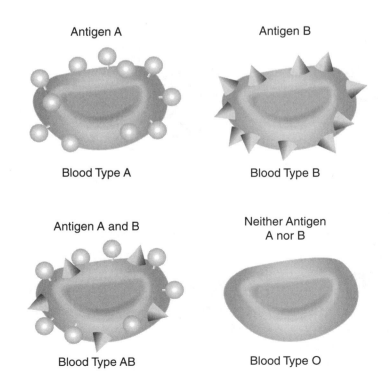

Antigen A

Blood Type A

Antigen B

Blood Type B

Antigen A and B

Blood Type AB

Neither Antigen
A nor B

Blood Type O

Blood Vessels

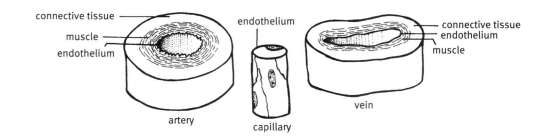

Blood vessels	Direction	Description	Type of blood	Valves
Arteries				
Veins				
Capillaries				

Heart

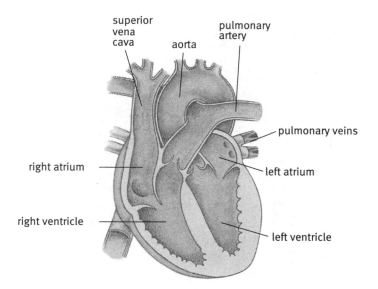

superior vena cava

aorta

pulmonary artery

pulmonary veins

right atrium

left atrium

right ventricle

left ventricle

Electrical Conduction

Respiratory System

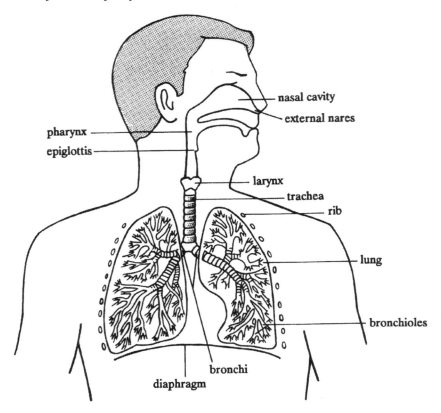

Ventilation

Practice Questions

4. After a person with B⁻ blood type is given a blood transfusion, hemolysis occurs. Which answer choice includes only blood types that will cause this reaction?

   A. AB^+, B^-, A^+
   B. AB^+, A^-, O^+
   C. AB^-, B^+, B^-
   D. B^+, O^-, A^+
   E. O^+, B^-, AB^-

5. A researcher wanting to study aerobic respiration in mammalian cells should not choose RBCs for her protocols because

   A. RBCs have a life span of only 120 days.
   B. aerobic respiration occurs only in the cells of alveoli.
   C. RBCs lack mitochondria and therefore attain their ATP anaerobically.
   D. RBCs consume O_2 at a faster rate than other cells.
   E. RBCs are much larger than other cells.

6. Which of the following is the correct sequence of the passages through which air travels during inhalation?

   A. Pharynx → trachea → lungs → bronchi → alveoli
   B. Larynx → pharynx → bronchi → lungs → alveoli
   C. Larynx → pharynx → trachea → bronchi → alveoli
   D. Pharynx → larynx → trachea → bronchi → alveoli
   E. Larynx → pharynx → bronchi → trachea → alveoli

Musculoskeletal System

Skeleton

Bone

Cartilage

Tendon

Ligament

Muscles

Muscle Types

Type	Striated	Nuclei	Voluntary
Skeletal			
Smooth			
Cardiac			

Sarcomere

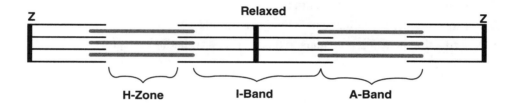

Relaxed

H-Zone   I-Band   A-Band

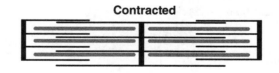

Contracted

Practice Questions

7. Which of the following statements about the musculoskeletal system is FALSE?

    A. Tendons join muscle to muscle; ligaments join muscle to bone.

    B. Contraction is initiated in muscle tissue by a cascade of Ca^{2+} ions.

    C. Specialized cells react to changing body conditions to maintain serum Ca^{2+} levels.

    D. The distance between Z lines always decreases during a contraction.

    E. The length of the H-zone always decreases during a contraction.

8. For most muscle groups, all of the following are required for a muscle to elongate EXCEPT one. Which of the following is the EXCEPTION?

    A. Influx of Ca^{2+} into that muscle's sarcoplasmic reticulum

    B. Consumption of ATP by that muscle

    C. Contraction of an antagonist muscle

    D. Elongation of actin filaments within that muscle

    E. Reduction in action potentials to that muscle's ryanodine receptors

9. If the calcium gradients of the sarcoplasmic reticulum were forced to dissipate, which immediate effect would be most likely?

    A. Emesis

    B. Hyperventilation

    C. Paralysis

    D. Relaxation

    E. Drowsiness

Nervous System

Neuron

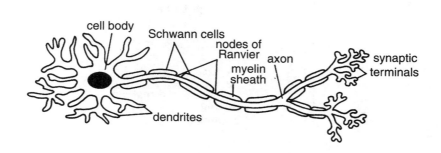

Dendrites

Cell Body

Axon

Synaptic Terminals

Myelin

Synapse

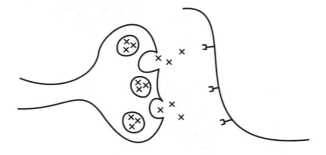

Action Potential

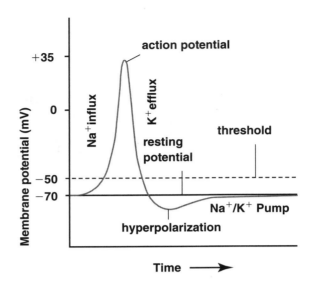

Nervous System Divisions

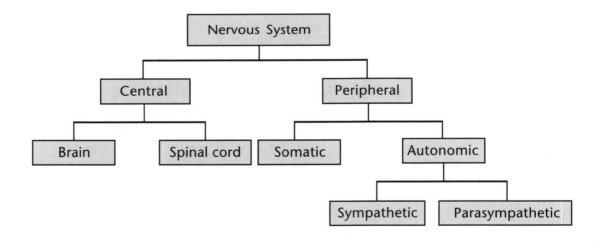

Practice Questions

10. Which of the following responses takes place upon activation of the parasympathetic nervous system?

    A.   Increased dilation of pupils
    B.   Increased heart rate
    C.   Increased respiratory rate
    D.   Decreased rate of digestion
    E.   Decreased blood flow to skeletal muscles

11. Below is a model of the simple nervous system of the sea snail, *Aplysia*.

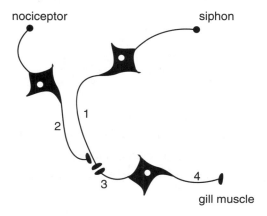

Which of the above point(s) indicates neural axons?

    A.   2 only
    B.   1 and 2 only
    C.   1 and 3 only
    D.   2, 3, and 4 only
    E.   1, 2, and 4 only

12. The absence of myelin on neurons would be most likely to result in

    A.   total paralysis.
    B.   uncoordinated movement of the limbs.
    C.   seizures.
    D.   increased risk of myocardial infarction.
    E.   frequent hyperventilation.

Practice Questions

13. After the learning process of habituation, neurons receiving a stimulus respond with less response than they would have prior to habituation. Which of the following effects of repeated stimulation is a possible explanation for habituation?

    A.   Permanent closure of calcium channels in the terminal membrane

    B.   Increase in the number of neurotransmitter receptors in the postsynaptic membrane

    C.   Decrease in the concentrations of neurotransmitter-degrading enzymes in the synapse

    D.   Neurotransmitter vesicles fusing with the terminal membrane in response to lower excitatory potentials

    E.   Increase in the amount of neurotransmitter released per action potential

14. Individual neurons in the skin containing mechanoreceptors can register the difference between a slight touch and a forceful push by

    A.   propagating a larger action potential due to a forceful push.

    B.   decreasing the voltage of the resting potential before a light touch.

    C.   releasing more frequent action potentials due to a forceful push.

    D.   releasing a higher concentration of neurotransmitters for a light touch.

    E.   increasing the time between action potentials due to a forceful push.

15. Sensitization allows neurons to respond more frequently to a stimulus than they would have prior to sensitization for a short period of time. What change in the axon terminal could explain this phenomenon?

    A.   The axon terminal is permanently hyperpolarized.

    B.   The axon terminal is permanently depolarized.

    C.   The axon terminal remains polarized longer following an action potential.

    D.   The axon terminal remains depolarized longer following an action potential.

    E.   The axon terminal releases less neurotransmitter following an action potential.

Endocrine System

Hypothalamus

Posterior Pituitary

Anterior Pituitary

Follicle-Stimulating Hormone (FSH)

Luteinizing Hormone (LH)

Adrenocorticotropic Hormone (ACTH)

Thyroid-Stimulating Hormone (TSH)

Prolactin

Endorphins

Growth Hormone

Thyroid

Triiodothyronine

Thyroxine

Calcitonin

Parathyroid

Parathyroid Hormone

Adrenal Cortex

Glucocorticoids

Mineralocorticoids

Adrenal Medulla

Epinephrine

Pancreas

Insulin

Glucagon

Testes

Androgens

Ovaries

Estrogen

Progesterone

Practice Questions

16. Which of the following accurately describes what happens after a meal high in sugar is eaten by a healthy human?

    A. Blood glucose concentration increases, insulin levels increase, cells take up glucose.
    B. Blood glucose concentration increases, glucagon levels increase, cells break down glycogen.
    C. Blood glucose levels normalize, insulin and glucagon levels both increase.
    D. Blood glucose concentration drops, glucagon levels increase, cells take up glucose.
    E. Blood glucose concentration drops, insulin levels increase, cells break down glycogen.

17. The function of parathyroid hormone is to

    A. stimulate osteoblasts to create new bone when serum calcium is low.
    B. stimulate osteoclasts to create new bone when serum calcium is high.
    C. stimulate osteoblasts to break down bone when serum calcium is low.
    D. stimulate osteoclasts to break down bone when serum calcium is low.
    E. stimulate osteoclasts to break down bone when serum calcium is high.

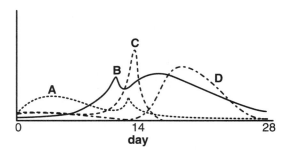

18. Which of the following lines in the chart above represents the levels of luteinizing hormone during the menstrual cycle?

    A. A
    B. B
    C. C
    D. D
    E. Both A and D

Urinary System

Kidney

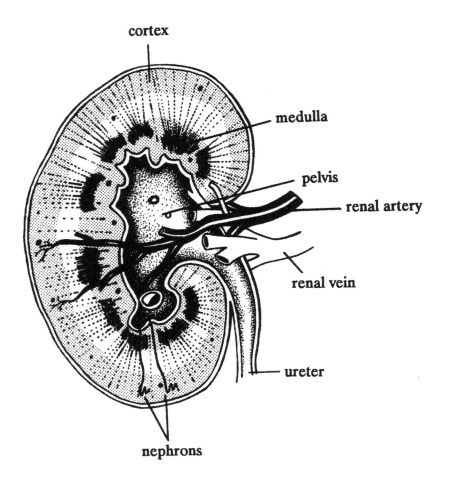

Nephron

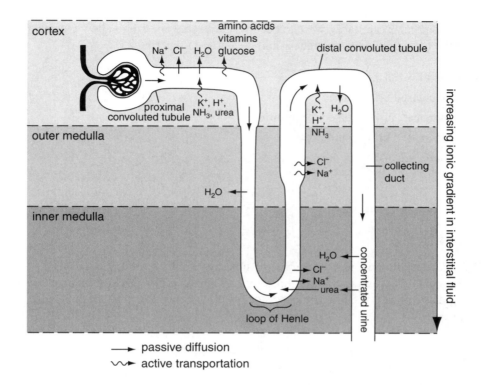

Filtration

Secretion

Reabsorption

Vasopressin (ADH)

Renin-Angiotensin-Aldosterone System

Practice Questions

19. If the glomerular capillaries were to become permeable enough to allow plasma proteins to enter the renal tubule, what effect would this have on the urine?

    A.   Increased urine output
    B.   Decreased urine output
    C.   Increased urine urea concentration
    D.   Decreased urine osmolarity
    E.   Increased urine salt concentration

20. Caffeine, as a diuretic, increases urine volume by inhibiting the action of ADH. Experimental data shows that administering an injection of ADH at the same time as caffeine counteracts the diuretic effects of caffeine, indicating that caffeine's mechanism of action is to

    A.   stimulate conversion of angiotensin-I into angiotensin-II.
    B.   block ADH receptors.
    C.   promote aldosterone secretion.
    D.   inhibit ADH secretion.
    E.   inhibit aldosterone secretion.

21. Which of the following is characteristic of the hormone vasopressin?

    A.   It increases water reabsorption in the kidneys.
    B.   It increases sodium reabsorption in the kidneys.
    C.   It increases waste reabsorption in the kidneys.
    D.   Its secretion is regulated by the hormone ACTH.
    E.   Its secretion is regulated by the enzyme renin.

Integumentary System

Skin

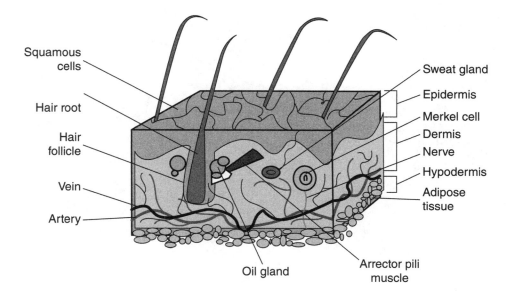

Acidity

Human Microbiome

Mucus

Mechanical Action

Blood Clotting

Immunological System

Immune Cells

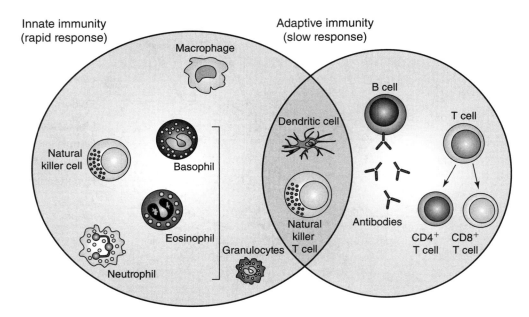

Granulocytes

Basophils/Mast Cells

Eosinophils

Neutrophils

Monocytes

Macrophages

Dendritic Cells

Lymphocytes

B Cells

T Cells

Natural Killer Cells

Practice Questions

22. An increase in serum eosinophil concentration would most likely indicate the presence of what type of agent?

    A.   Bacteria

    B.   Fungus

    C.   Parasite

    D.   Venom

    E.   Virus

23. Which of the following is NOT involved in nonspecific immune defense?

    A.   Skin

    B.   Lysozymes

    C.   Interferons

    D.   Macrophages

    E.   B cells

24. The main function of $CD8^+$ T cells is to

    A.   promote an allergic response.

    B.   stimulate other immune cells.

    C.   release antibodies.

    D.   destroy damaged cells.

    E.   present antigens.

Reproductive System

Male Reproductive Anatomy

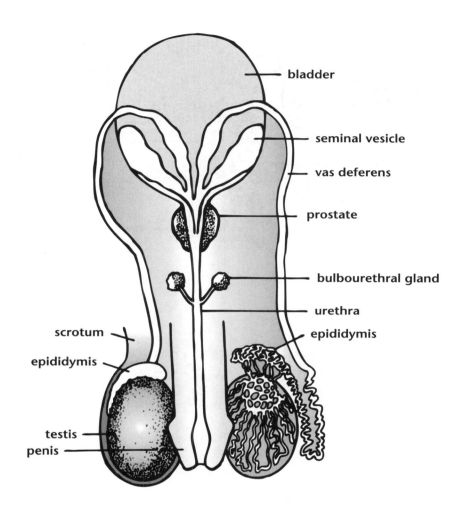

- bladder
- seminal vesicle
- vas deferens
- prostate
- bulbourethral gland
- urethra
- epididymis
- scrotum
- epididymis
- testis
- penis

Female Reproductive Anatomy

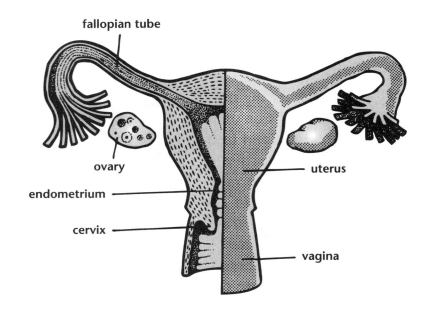

Practice Questions

25. Which of the following is FALSE with regard to the reproductive system?

    A.   Fertilization of the egg takes places in the oviduct.
    B.   The function of the ductus deferens is to store sperm.
    C.   The function of the epididymis is to store sperm.
    D.   The bulbourethral gland is present in the male reproductive system.
    E.   Eggs are released by the ovarian follicle during ovulation.

26. Which of the following structures is found in both male and female systems?

    A.   Epididymis
    B.   Fallopian tubes
    C.   Testes
    D.   Urethra
    E.   Uterus

27. Which of the following hormones does NOT promote production and development of sperm?

    A.   Follicle-stimulating hormone
    B.   Testosterone
    C.   Luteinizing hormone
    D.   Gonadotropin-releasing hormone
    E.   Somatostatin

Cell and Molecular Biology

Mitosis and Meiosis

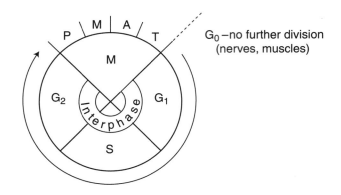

G_0 – no further division
(nerves, muscles)

Cell Cycle

Gap

Synthesis

Mitosis

Meiosis

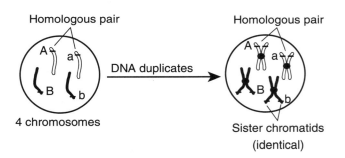

Homologous pair

DNA duplicates

4 chromosomes

Homologous pair

Sister chromatids
(identical)

Cellular Machinery

Chromatid

Centromere

Centriole

Centrosome

Stages of Mitosis and Meiosis

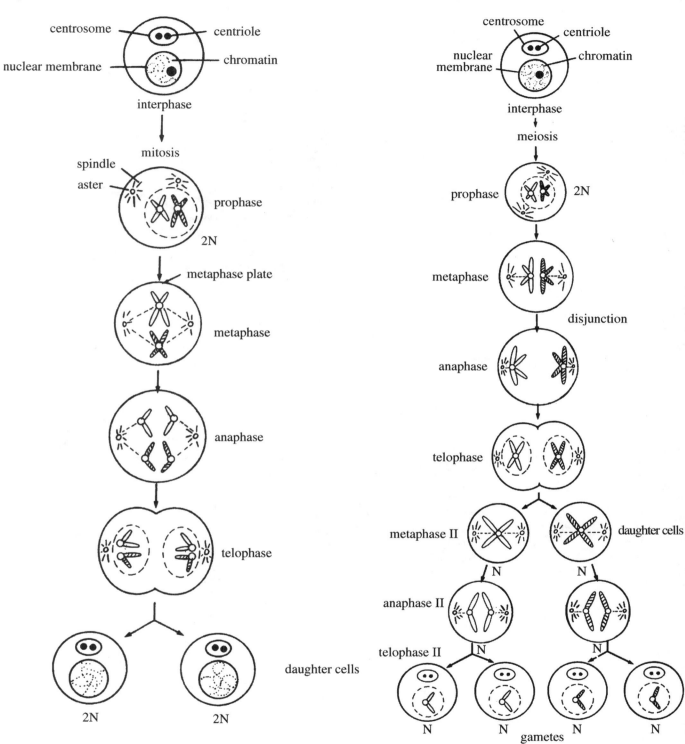

Fertilization

Spermatogenesis

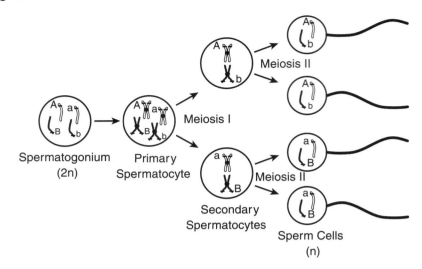

Oogenesis

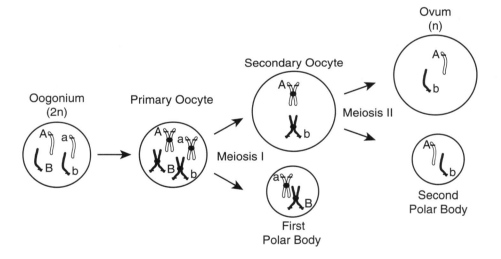

Practice Questions

28. After the age of 35, women experience a dramatic increase in the rate of nondisjunction, centromeres not separating correctly during meiosis. This results in

   A. total infertility.
   B. an increased likelihood of birthing identical twins.
   C. a decreased ability to have male children.
   D. a decreased chance of fertilization.
   E. an increased probability of forming zygotes with an incorrect number of chromosomes.

29. A mutation has occurred in one chromosome of a spermatogonium. This mutation will show up in how many of the gametes produced from this cell?

   A. None
   B. One
   C. Two
   D. Four
   E. Cannot be determined

30. Each stage of the cell cycle is regulated by proteins coded for by suppressor genes that control the rate of cell division. Mutations to these genes are direct risk factors for

   A. insomnia.
   B. myocardial infarction.
   C. diabetes mellitus.
   D. cancer.
   E. osteoporosis.

Developmental Biology

Descriptive Embryology

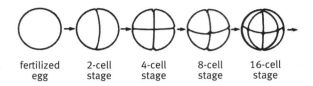

fertilized egg → 2-cell stage → 4-cell stage → 8-cell stage → 16-cell stage →

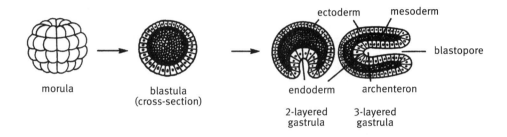

morula → blastula (cross-section) →

ectoderm   mesoderm

blastopore

endoderm   archenteron

2-layered gastrula   3-layered gastrula

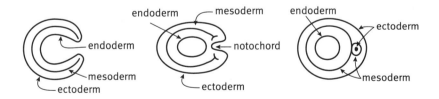

endoderm

mesoderm

endoderm

endoderm — mesoderm

ectoderm

mesoderm — notochord

ectoderm

Developmental Mechanisms

Totipotent Cells

Germ Layers

Ectoderm

Mesoderm

Endoderm

Induction

STUDY TIP

Developmental biology has less content to learn than some other subject areas but is still worth four points on Test Day. Learn this material well to maximize your studying efficiency!

Practice Questions

31. Which of the following is the most likely mechanism for the formation of fraternal twins?

   A.   Splitting of a 2-cell or 4-cell embryo into two organisms
   B.   Collapse of a blastula into two organisms
   C.   Two sperm fertilizing one ovum
   D.   Two sperm fertilizing two ova
   E.   One sperm fertilizing two ova

32. Individuals with a certain disorder are known to have a reduced ability to sweat, sparse body and scalp hair, and vision defects due to an abnormality arising in the

   A.   ectoderm.
   B.   endoderm.
   C.   mesoderm.
   D.   morula.
   E.   blastocyst.

33. Spina bifida (myelomeningocele) is a birth defect involving the back and spinal cord caused by a problem first arising in the

   A.   zygote.
   B.   morula.
   C.   blastocyst.
   D.   neurula.
   E.   fetus.

Study Plan

After Class: Biology 2

| Complete Remaining *Lesson Book* Practice Questions | 30m | |
| Practice with Tests and Quizzes | | |

Before Class: Perceptual Ability 2

| Read *Review Notes* Chapter 64 | 30m | |

PERCEPTUAL ABILITY 2

TOPICS COVERED

- Reviewing Practice Tests
- Goal Setting
- Angle Ranking
- Hole Punching
- Cube Counting
- Keyholes
- Top-Front-End
- Pattern Folding

After this session you will be able to:

- Recall the specific rules of Angle Ranking, Hole Punching, and Cube Counting questions
- Apply relevant strategies to solve Angle Ranking, Hole Punching, and Cube Counting questions
- Recognize the unique features of each Perceptual Ability subsection

Reviewing Your Practice Tests

Review Every Answer

Track Changed Answers

Check Your Pacing

Complete Why I Missed It Charts

Section	Q #	Topic or type	Why I missed it
Biology	4	Embryology	Didn't know content
Quant	17	Algebra	Solved for x instead of $x + 2$
RC	29	Detail Question	Did not go back to passage

Goal Setting

Calendar Revision

Complete any remaining Unit 1 assignments

Recalculate time remaining until Test Day

Build in time to take additional Full-Length tests

Achieving Your Test Day Goals

Practice

Goals by Section

Overall Goals

PAT Section Structure

60 minutes for 90 questions

15 questions per subsection

Subsection Order:

Keyholes

Top-Front-End

Angle Ranking

Hole Punching

Cube Counting

Pattern Folding

Angle Ranking

PART 3

Each question in this section presents four INTERIOR angles, labeled 1 through 4. Examine the four interior angles presented in each question.

Rank each question's angles in order from smallest to largest. Select the answer choice that represents the correct ranking. Try the following example:

Example

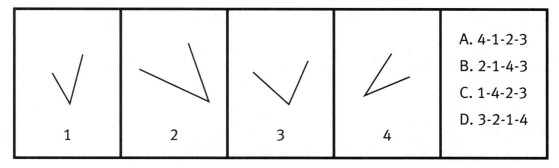

A. 4-1-2-3

B. 2-1-4-3

C. 1-4-2-3

D. 3-2-1-4

The correct ranking of the angles from small to large is 4-1-2-3. Therefore, the correct answer is choice (A).

Proceed to Questions

PERCEPTUAL ABILITY 2

Overview

Four angles are given and must be ranked in order of increasing angle.

The Rules

Each question contains four interior angles that are distinct from each other. There will always be at least a one to three degree difference between sequentially ranked angles.

Strategies

Smallest and Largest Angles

Blocking

Stacking

Practice Questions

1.

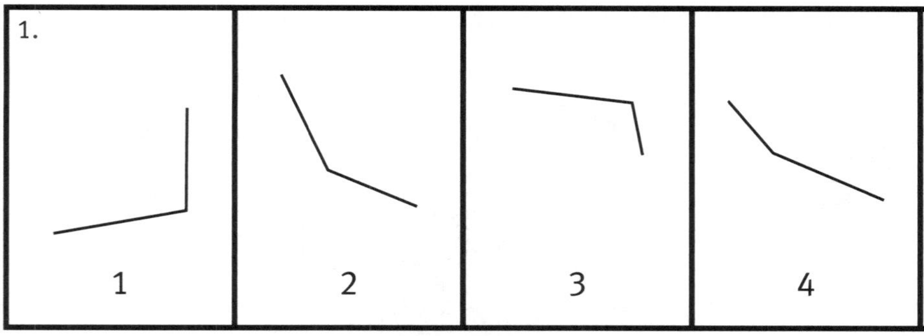

| 1 | 2 | 3 | 4 | A. 3-1-2-4
B. 3-1-4-2
C. 1-3-2-4
D. 1-3-4-2 |

2.

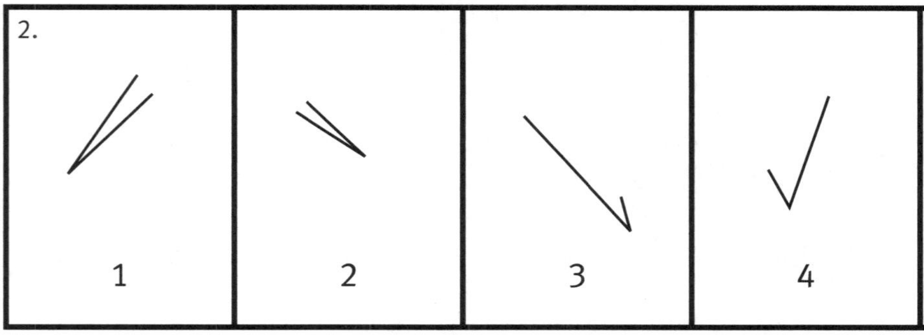

| 1 | 2 | 3 | 4 | A. 2-3-4-1
B. 2-1-3-4
C. 1-4-3-2
D. 4-3-1-2 |

3.

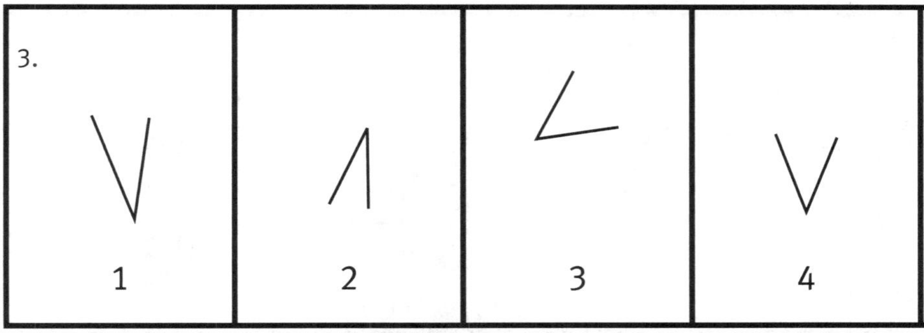

| 1 | 2 | 3 | 4 | A. 2-1-4-3
B. 2-3-4-1
C. 2-4-1-3
D. 1-2-3-4 |

4.

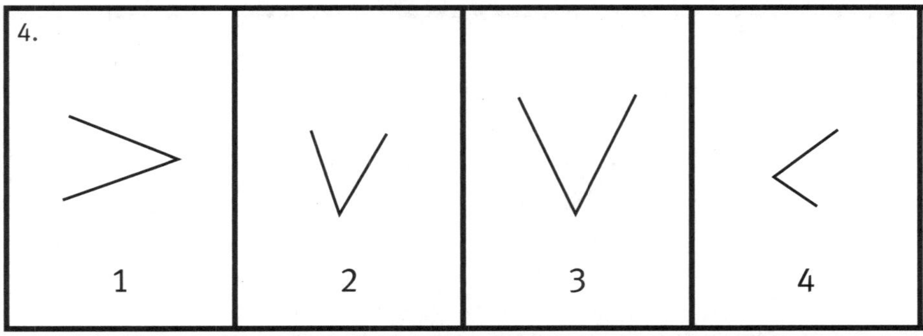

| 1 | 2 | 3 | 4 | A. 1-3-4-2
B. 1-2-4-3
C. 2-1-3-4
D. 1-2-3-4 |

Practice Questions

5.				A. 1-2-3-4
1	2	3	4	B. 2-1-3-4
				C. 2-1-4-3
				D. 1-4-2-3

6.				A. 4-1-3-2
1	2	3	4	B. 2-3-4-1
				C. 1-4-2-3
				D. 1-4-3-2

7.				A. 1-3-2-4
1	2	3	4	B. 3-1-2-4
				C. 3-1-4-2
				D. 1-3-4-2

8.				A. 1-3-2-4
1	2	3	4	B. 1-2-3-4
				C. 3-1-2-4
				D. 3-2-1-4

Hole Punching

PART 4

In these questions, a flat, square piece of paper is folded one or more times. Broken lines indicate the original position of the paper, and solid lines indicate the position of the folded paper. The folded paper remains within the boundaries of the original, flat sheet. The paper is not turned or twisted. There are one, two, or three folds per question.

After the final fold is performed, a hole is punched in the paper. Once the hole is punched, mentally unfold the paper and determine the position(s) of the hole(s) on the original flat sheet.

Select the answer choice that represents the same pattern of dark circles that would reflect the position of holes on the unfolded sheet. There is only one correct pattern for each question. Try the following example:

Example

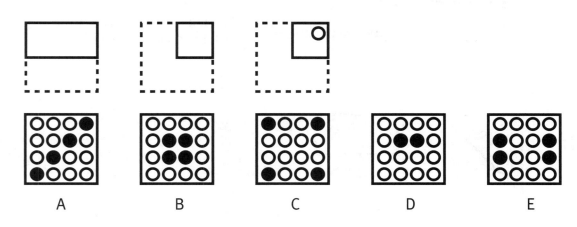

A	B	C	D	E

The correct answer is choice (C).

Proceed to Questions

Overview

You must identify where the holes punched in a folded piece of paper will be when the piece of paper is unfolded.

The Rules

A flat, square piece of paper is folded one or more times.

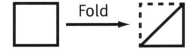

Broken lines indicate the original position of the paper, and solid lines indicate the position of the folded paper. The folded paper remains within the boundaries of the original, flat sheet. The paper is not turned or twisted.

Where paper is.

Where paper was.

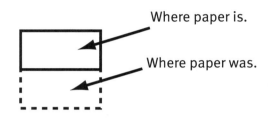

Determine how the paper was folded by looking at its position before and after the fold.

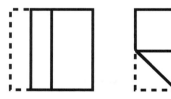

These are some possible first folds.

There are one, two, or three folds per question.

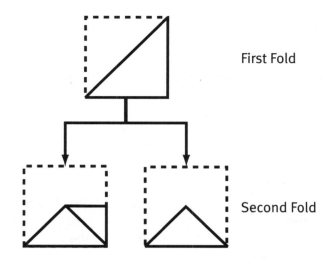

First Fold

Here are two of the many possible second folds following the given first fold.

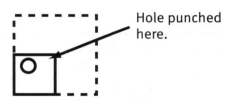

Second Fold

After the final fold is performed, one or more holes are punched in the paper. Once the holes are punched, mentally unfold the paper and ascertain the positions of the holes on the original flat sheet.

Hole punched here.

Notice that the location of the hole being punched is indicated by the outline of a circle.

The location of the hole punched is constrained by the fact that no "half" holes are generated. However, a hole may be punched along a fold so that when the paper is unfolded, a single "whole" hole results from the "half" punch.

Strategies

First Fold Line of Symmetry

The first fold is particularly important for determining the symmetry of the final solution.

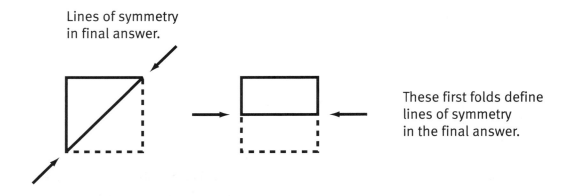

Lines of symmetry in final answer.

These first folds define lines of symmetry in the final answer.

Practice with Lines of Symmetry

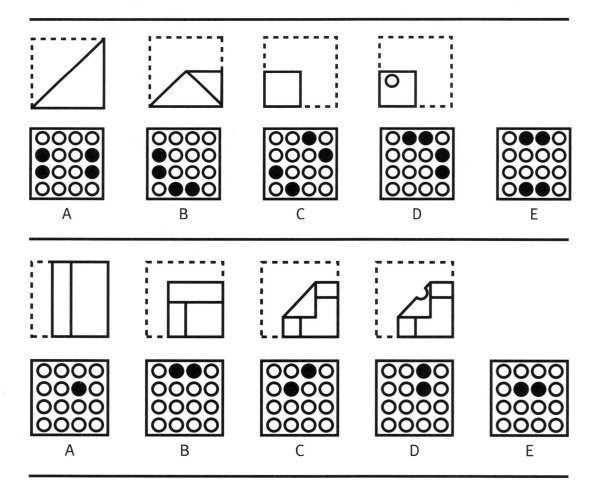

Number of Holes

Practice with Number of Holes

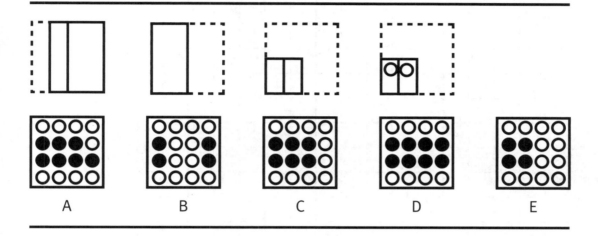

Position

Practice with Position

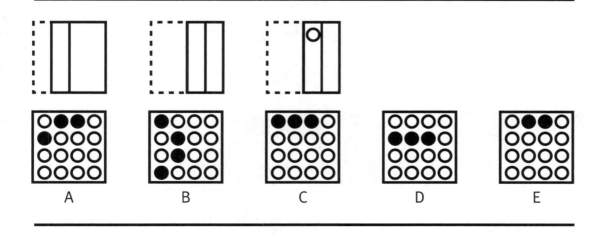

Scratch Paper Strategy

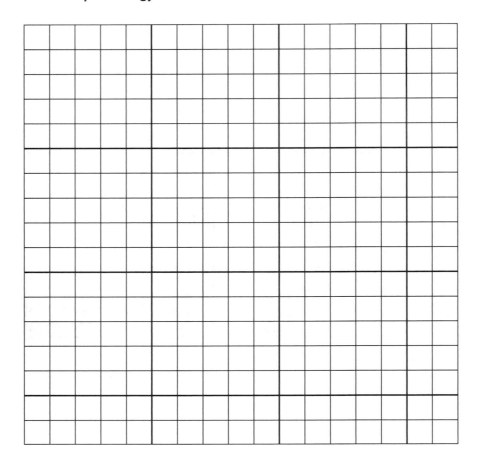

Practice Questions

9.

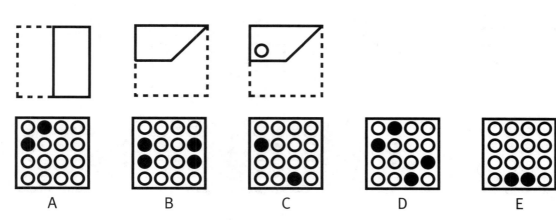

10.

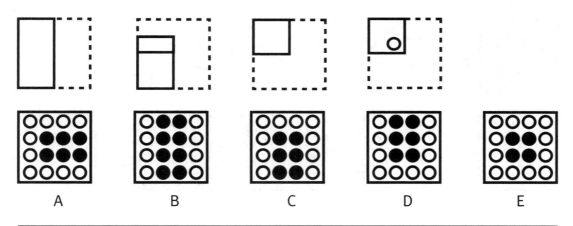

Practice Questions

11.

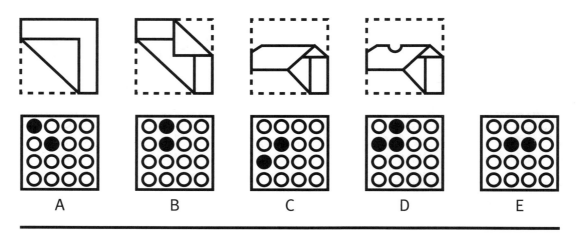

12.

Practice Questions

13.

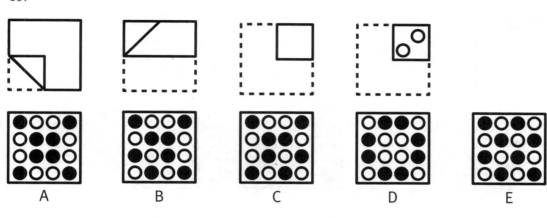

14.

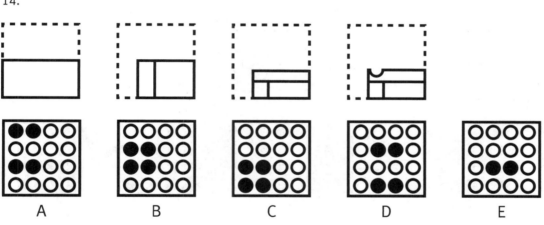

. **Practice Questions**

15.

A	B	C	D	E

16.

A	B	C	D	E

Cube Counting

PART 5

Each figure presented in this section has been constructed by cementing together identical cubes. After being cemented, each figure was painted on all sides EXCEPT for the bottom (the side on which the figure rests). The only hidden cubes are the ones necessary to support other cubes in the figure.

Examine each figure carefully regarding the number of sides on each cube that have been painted. The following questions ask for this information. Select the correct answer choice from the ones provided. Try the following example:

Example

In the Example Figure, how many cubes have two of their exposed sides painted?

A. 1 cube
B. 2 cubes
C. 3 cubes
D. 4 cubes
E. 5 cubes

Example Figure

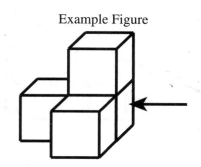

The correct answer is choice A. The cube is indicated with an arrow above.

Proceed to Questions

Overview

A stack of cubes is given. You must determine how many cubes have a particular number of exposed sides.

The Rules

Each figure has been constructed by cementing together identical cubes.

After being cemented, each figure was painted on all sides EXCEPT for the bottom (the side on which the figure rests).

The only hidden cubes are the ones necessary to support other cubes in the figure.

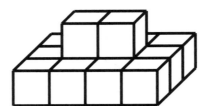

How many cubes are in this stack?

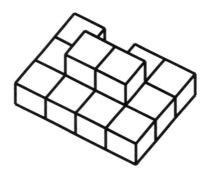

This is how you should interpret the stack of cubes shown above.

The Six Cubes of the PAT

One-Sider

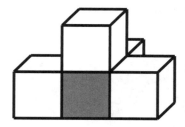

The One-Sider usually appears on the faces of complex figures.

Two-Sider

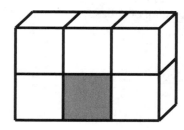

The Two-Sider can appear on the bottoms of walls.

Three-Sider

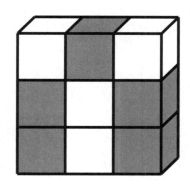

The Three-Sider can appear in many places, including on the edges of a wall of cubes.

Four-Sider

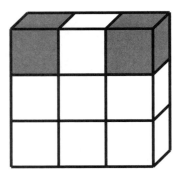

The Four-Sider appears on the corners of a wall of cubes.

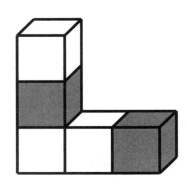

The Four-Sider can also appear within a column of cubes.

Five-Sider

The cube with five sides exposed can only appear in the following way:

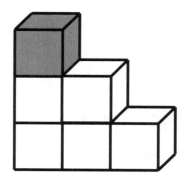

The Five-Sider sits above all immediate surrounding blocks.

No-Sider

The cube with no exposed side can only appear in the following way:

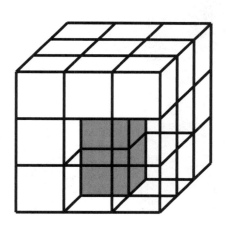

The No-Sider must be completely surrounded by cubes and/or the floor.

Tallying the Cubes

Figure A

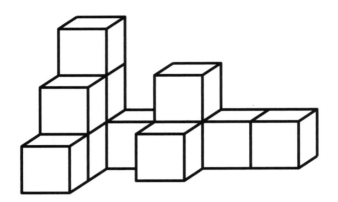

Sides	#
0	
1	
2	
3	
4	
5	
Total	

Practice Questions

17. In Figure A, how many cubes have two of their exposed sides painted?

    A.   1 cube
    B.   2 cubes
    C.   3 cubes
    D.   4 cubes
    E.   5 cubes

18. In Figure A, how many cubes have four of their exposed sides painted?

    A.   1 cube
    B.   2 cubes
    C.   3 cubes
    D.   4 cubes
    E.   5 cubes

19. In Figure A, how many cubes have five of their exposed sides painted?

    A.   1 cube
    B.   2 cubes
    C.   3 cubes
    D.   4 cubes
    E.   5 cubes

Figure B

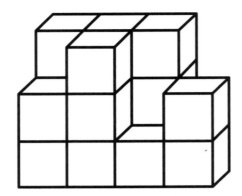

20. In Figure B, how many cubes have one of their exposed sides painted?

    A.   1 cube
    B.   2 cubes
    C.   3 cubes
    D.   4 cubes
    E.   5 cubes

21. In Figure B, how many cubes have three of their exposed sides painted?

    A.   1 cube
    B.   2 cubes
    C.   3 cubes
    D.   4 cubes
    E.   5 cubes

22. In Figure B, how many cubes have five of their exposed sides painted?

    A.   1 cube
    B.   2 cubes
    C.   3 cubes
    D.   4 cubes
    E.   5 cubes

Practice Questions

Figure C

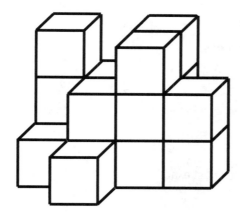

23. In Figure C, how many cubes have one of their exposed sides painted?

   A.   1 cube
   B.   2 cubes
   C.   3 cubes
   D.   4 cubes
   E.   5 cubes

24. In Figure C, how many cubes have three of their exposed sides painted?

   A.   1 cube
   B.   2 cubes
   C.   3 cubes
   D.   4 cubes
   E.   5 cubes

25. In Figure C, how many cubes have four of their exposed sides painted?

   A.   1 cube
   B.   2 cubes
   C.   3 cubes
   D.   4 cubes
   E.   5 cubes

Keyholes

Rules

1. Objects can pass through in any of 6 possible directions.

2. Objects cannot be rotated or turned after they have been inserted.

3. The opening must match the external outline of the object exactly.

4. The size of the opening must match the size of the object.

5. There are no hidden irregularities in the object.

Strategies

Practice Questions

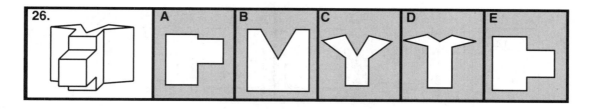

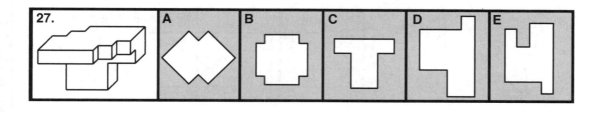

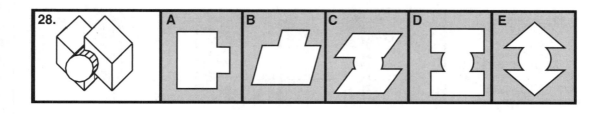

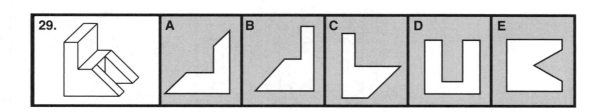

Practice Questions

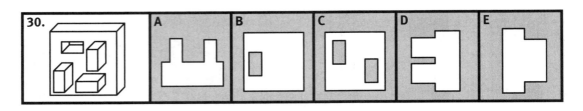

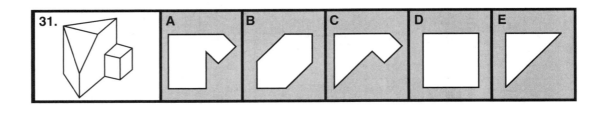

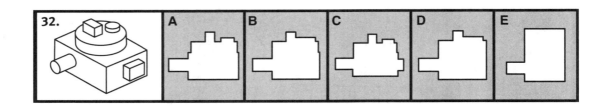

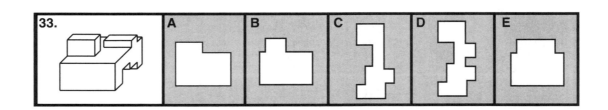

Top-Front-End

Rules

1. There are 3 possible views of the object, and one of them is missing.

2. The views of the object are orthogonal.

3. In the question stem the front is always on the bottom left, the top is always on the top left, and the end view is always on the bottom right.

4. The end view of the object is always from the right.

5. Solid lines represent features of the object that are visible from a given view; dotted lines are hidden from a given view.

Strategies

Practice Questions

34. Choose the correct **FRONT VIEW**.

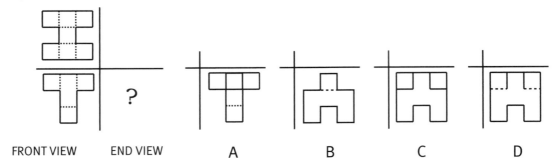

35. Choose the correct **TOP VIEW**.

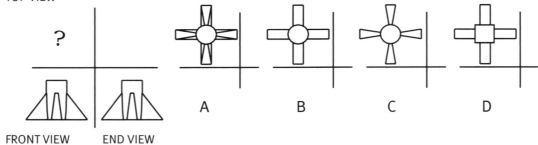

Practice Questions

36. Choose the correct **END VIEW**.

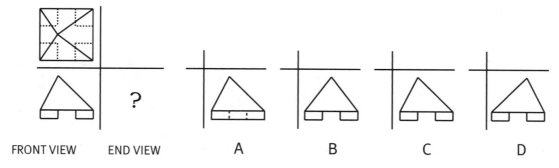

37. Choose the correct **TOP VIEW**.

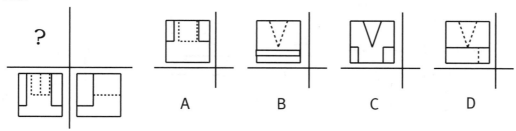

Practice Questions

38. Choose the correct **END VIEW**.

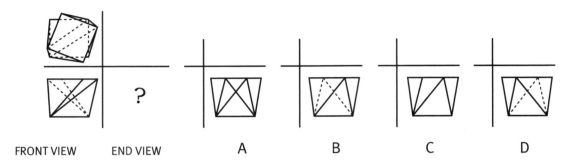

39. Choose the correct **TOP VIEW**.

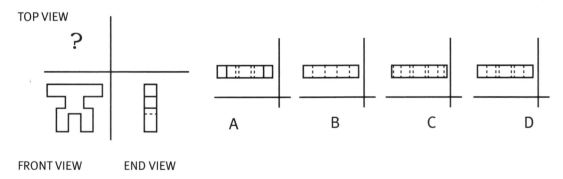

Practice Questions

40. Choose the correct **TOP VIEW**.

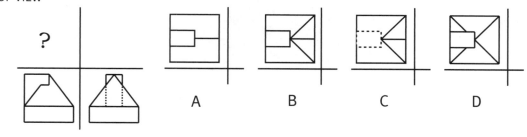

A   B   C   D

41. Choose the correct **FRONT VIEW**.

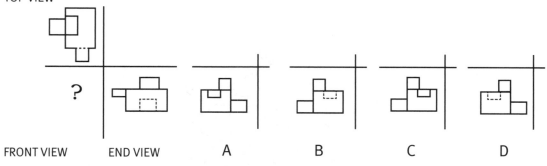

A   B   C   D

Top-Front-End 3D Images

Pattern Folding

34.

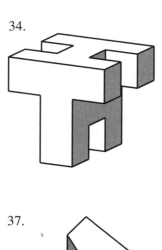

35.

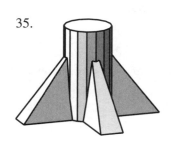

36.

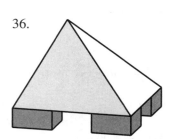

37.

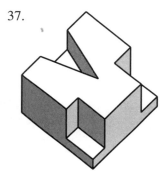

38.

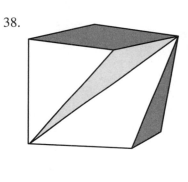

39.

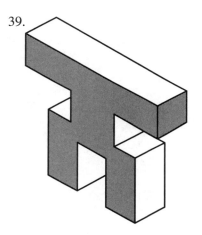

40.

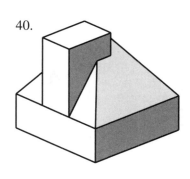

41.

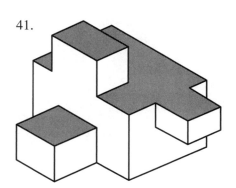

Rules

1. A flat pattern with folds indicated is given.

2. The pattern must be folded into the page to produce the correct 3-dimensional object.

3. The correct answer may be any view of the 3-dimensional object.

Strategies

Practice Questions

42.

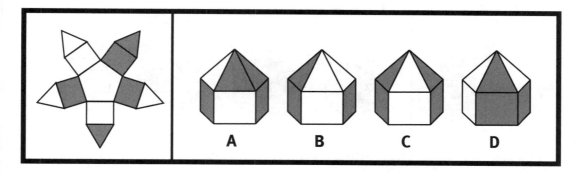

43.

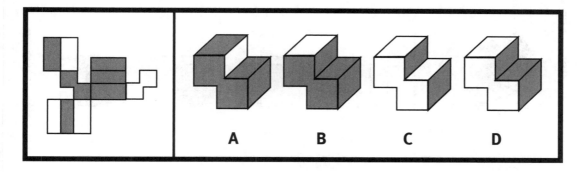

44.

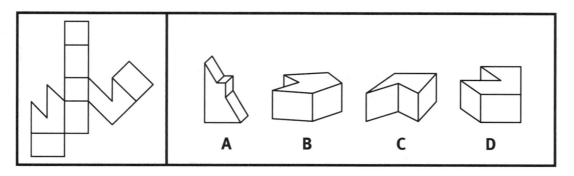

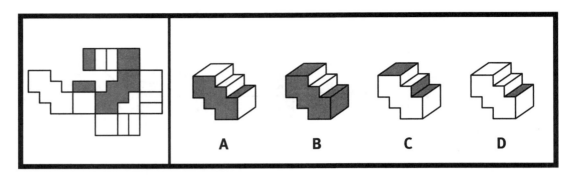

Practice Questions

45.

46.

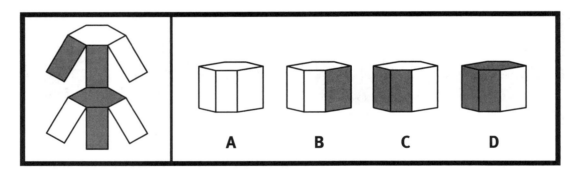

47.

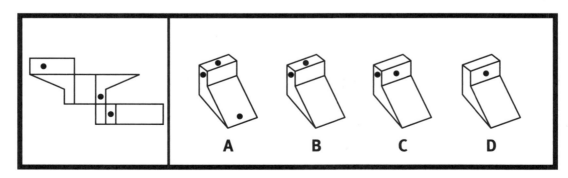

Practice Questions

48.

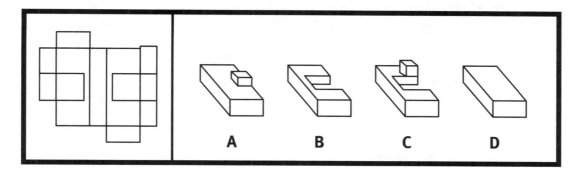

49.

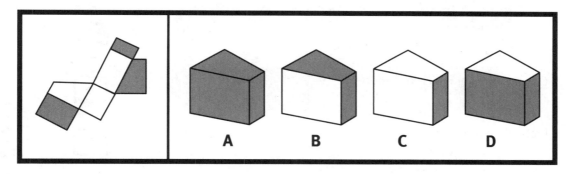

Study Plan

After Class: Perceptual Ability 2

Complete Remaining *Lesson Book* Practice Questions	30m	
Practice with Tests and Quizzes		

Before Class: Quantitative Reasoning 2

Read *Review Notes* Chapters 58–62	1h 30m	
Graphical Analysis and Coordinate Geometry Video	5m	
Data Interpretation Video	5m	
Volume Video	5m	
Classic Math Formulas Workshop	45m	
Probability Workshop	45m	
Combinations and Permutations Workshop	45m	
Geometry Basics Workshop	45m	
Word Problems Workshop	45m	
Common Conversion Factors		PDF

QUANTITATIVE REASONING 2

TOPICS COVERED

- Kaplan Strategic Math Review
- Conversions
- Probability and Statistics
- Geometry
- Trigonometry

After this session you will be able to:

- Calculate conversions
- Calculate averages, variance, and standard deviation
- Calculate probabilities
- Analyze geometric shapes
- Calculate trigonometric relationships

Kaplan Strategic Math Review

Traditional Math

Picking Numbers

Backsolving

Estimation

Educated Guessing

Strategic Math Exercises

Match each of the following question stems with any strategies that would be useful for solving the problem.

Question stem	Strategy				
	Traditional Math	Picking Numbers	Back-solving	Estimation	Strategic Guessing
$(\sqrt{3} + \sqrt{7})(\sqrt{3} - \sqrt{7}) =$	X				
Three students are competing to collect the most stamps. They collect 103, 198, and 295 stamps, respectively. What is the average number of stamps collected per student?				X	X
During a sale, a store sells 20% of its remaining stock each day, without replenishment. After 4 days, what fraction of its original stock has it sold?		X			
A truck driver drove for 2 days. On the second day he drove 3 hours longer and at an average speed of 15 miles per hour faster than he drove on the first day. If he drove a total of 1,020 miles and spent 21 hours driving during the 2 days, what was his average speed on the first day?				X	X
Of the 150 employees at a company, 80 are full time and 100 have worked at the company for at least a year. There are 20 employees who aren't full time and haven't worked at the company for at least a year. How many full-time employees of this company have worked at the company for at least a year?			X		

TEST DAY TIP

If you start using one strategy and get stuck, consider if there is another strategy you can use instead. Most questions can be solved in multiple ways.

Conversions

Conversion questions ask you to switch between units of temperature, time, weight, or distance. Set up conversion problems so that units cancel out with each successive ratio. This means that conversion problems require careful attention to scratch work.

Example:

1. Approximately how many feet are in 65 meters? (There are 5,280 feet in one mile and 0.62 miles in one kilometer.)

    A.   53 feet
    B.   213 feet
    C.   780 feet
    D.   3,273 feet
    E.   5,535 feet

TEST DAY TIP

Conversion questions are a great way to get points quickly on Test Day, but make sure to take the time to set up your scratch work so you don't make careless mistakes.

Practice Questions

2. Two quarts equal 1.89 liters, and 1 liter equals 1 cubic decimeter. Therefore, how many cubic centimeters are in 1 gallon?

   A. 3.78 cm^3
   B. 378 cm^3
   C. 3,780 cm^3
   D. 4,780 cm^3
   E. 7,560 cm^3

3. If the conversion between degrees Celsius (C) to degrees Fahrenheit (F) can be represented by the equation $C = \frac{5}{9}(F - 32)$, what temperature in degrees Fahrenheit is equivalent to 24°C?

   A. −4.40
   B. 13.3
   C. 43.2
   D. 45.3
   E. 75.2

4. Magnabulk Corp sells boxes holding d magnets each. The boxes are shipped in crates, each holding b boxes. What is the price charged per magnet (in cents) if Magnabulk charges m dollars for each crate?

   A. $\dfrac{100bd}{m}$
   B. $\dfrac{100m}{bd}$
   C. $\dfrac{bd}{100m}$
   D. $\dfrac{m}{bd}$
   E. $\dfrac{100b}{m}$

Probability and Statistics

Statistics

Mean

The mean, or average, is the sum of all the members of a data set divided by the number of items in that data set.

$$\text{Mean} = \frac{\text{Sum of terms}}{\text{Number of terms}}$$

Median

The median is the center number in a data set arranged in numerical order.

Mode

The mode is the most common number in a set.

Example:

5. What are the mean, median, and mode of the data set below?

7, 11, 9, 7, 11, 8, 11, 6, 47

Mean:

Median:

Mode:

Practice Questions

6.
$$\{93, 101, 102, 100, 110\}$$

<u>Quantity A</u>

The mean of the data set

<u>Quantity B</u>

The median of the data set

A.   Quantity A is greater.
B.   Quantity B is greater.
C.   The two quantities are equal.
D.   The relationship cannot be determined from the information given.

7. The mean of all the scores on a certain algebra test was 90. If the average score of the 8 seniors taking the test was 87 and the average score of all the juniors taking the test was 92, then how many juniors took the test?

A.   5
B.   8
C.   10
D.   12
E.   15

8.   Which of the following is the mean of n, $n + 2$, and $n + 7$?

A. n
B. $n + 3$
C. $n + 9$
D. $3n + 9$
E. $\dfrac{(3n + 9)}{5}$

Variance

Variance, σ^2, is one way to measure the dispersion of data.

$$\sigma^2 = \frac{1}{n}\sum_{i=1}^{n}\left(x_i - \overline{x}\right)^2$$

Use the following steps to calculate variance:

1. Find the mean of the data.

2. Subtract the mean from each of the numbers in the data set.

3. Square each of the results from step 2.

4. Take the average of the numbers from step 3.

Since Variance problems are highly repetitive, using a chart to fill in the values at each step simplifies the calculations and minimizes the chance for error:

Find the average for the set, $\overline{x}$:

i	$(i-\overline{x})$	$(i-\overline{x})^2$

Sum of squared differences:

Average (divide by number of terms):

Standard Deviation

Standard deviation, σ, is the square root of variance. Standard deviation can also be thought of as a measure of the average distance of each number from the overall mean of the number set. To calculate standard deviation, complete the steps above for variance and then perform a final step of taking the square root of the result.

$$\sigma = \sqrt{\frac{1}{n}\sum_{i=1}^{n}\left(x_i - \bar{x}\right)^2}$$

The 68–95–99.7 rule can be applied to a normally distributed set of data. If the numbers in a data set are normally distributed: 68% of the data lie within 1 standard deviation of the mean, 95% of the data lie within 2 standard deviations of the mean, and 99.7% of the data lie within 3 standard deviations of the mean.

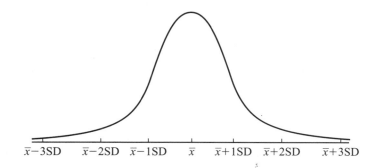

$$\bar{x}-3\text{SD} \quad \bar{x}-2\text{SD} \quad \bar{x}-1\text{SD} \quad \bar{x} \quad \bar{x}+1\text{SD} \quad \bar{x}+2\text{SD} \quad \bar{x}+3\text{SD}$$

Example:

9. What are the variance and standard deviation of the data set shown below?

   {4, 5, 8, 10, 13}

   A. $8, \sqrt{8}$

   B. $9, 3$

   C. $\frac{54}{5}, \sqrt{\frac{54}{5}}$

   D. $11, \sqrt{11}$

   E. $16, 4$

Practice Questions

10. The mean weight of men aged 70 to 79 in North America is approximately 75 kg, with a standard deviation of 12 kg. Assuming a normal distribution, which best represents the minimum weight of a male in the top 5% by weight of men in their 70s?

    A. 87 kg
    B. 96 kg
    C. 99 kg
    D. 105 kg
    E. 111 kg

11. $\{5, 9, 12, 18, 21\}$

Quantity A	Quantity B
The range of the data	The standard deviation of the data

    A. Quantity A is greater.
    B. Quantity B is greater.
    C. The two quantities are equal.
    D. The relationship cannot be determined from the information given.

12. What is the standard deviation of the sample: 1, 2, 2, 4, 6?

    A. $\sqrt{\dfrac{8}{5}}$
    B. $\sqrt{3}$
    C. $\sqrt{\dfrac{16}{5}}$
    D. $\sqrt{\dfrac{17}{5}}$
    E. $\sqrt{\dfrac{19}{5}}$

Graphical Representations of Data

Data on the DAT may be given in a list, table, or graph. If in a table or chart, data should be treated the same way as if in a list.

Example:

The chart and the table display the same data in two different ways:

Trial	Outcome
1	1
2	3
3	4
4	1
5	1
6	2
7	5
8	4
9	5
10	4

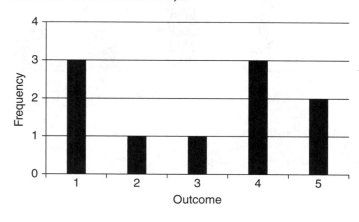

13. Given the data above, what are the mean and median of that data?

   A.   mean: 3; median: 3.5
   B.   mean: 3.5; median: 3
   C.   mean: 3; median: 4
   D.   mean: 3.5; median: 4.5
   E.   mean: 5.5; median: 5

Practice Questions

Use the chart below to answer the following questions.

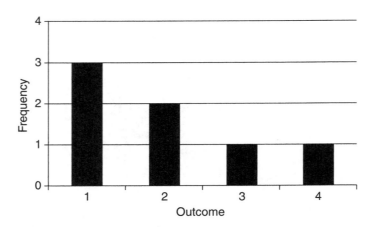

14. What is the mean of the data?

    A. 1
    B. 2
    C. 3
    D. 4
    E. 5

15. What is the median of the data?

    A. 1
    B. 2
    C. 3
    D. 4
    E. 5

16. What is the standard deviation of the data?

    A. $\sqrt{\dfrac{3}{5}}$

    B. $\sqrt{\dfrac{11}{16}}$

    C. $\sqrt{\dfrac{4}{5}}$

    D. 1

    E. $\sqrt{\dfrac{8}{7}}$

Probability

Probability $= \dfrac{\text{Number of desired outcomes}}{\text{Total number of outcomes}}$

The sum of the probabilities of a complete set of mutually exclusive possible outcomes is 1.

To find the probability that one *OR* another of two mutually exclusive events occurs, *ADD* the probabilities of the two events.

Example:

When rolling a single die, what is the probability of rolling either a 1 or a 3?

1 and 3

$\frac{1}{6} \times \frac{1}{6}$

To find the probability that one *AND* another of two independent events occurs, *MULTIPLY* the probabilities of the two events.

Example:

Two dice are being rolled. What is the probability of rolling a 3 on the first die and a 3 on the second die?

To find the probability of *AT LEAST* some number of events occurring, find the probability that those events do not occur and subtract from one.

Example:

When rolling 2 dice, what is the probability of at least one die rolling a 3?

If objects are being removed from a set in a given problem, establish whether or not they are being replaced prior to setting up your calculation.

Example:

17. A bowl contains only 5 bananas and 5 apples. If one piece of fruit is selected from the bowl at random and a second piece is selected from the bowl without replacing the first, what is the probability that both pieces of fruit chosen are apples?

A. $\frac{1}{10}$

B. $\frac{1}{5}$

C. $\frac{2}{9}$

D. $\frac{1}{4}$

E. $\frac{2}{5}$

Practice Questions

18. Robert tossed a fair coin 3 times. What is the probability that the coin landed heads up exactly twice?

    A. 0.125
    B. 0.250
    C. 0.375
    D. 0.500
    E. 0.750

19. All of the marbles in a bag are blue, red, or green. If a marble is withdrawn from the bag at random, the probability that it is blue is $\frac{3}{5}$ and the probability that it is red is $\frac{1}{10}$. What is the probability that a marble withdrawn from the bag is green?

    A. $\frac{3}{50}$
    B. $\frac{3}{10}$
    C. $\frac{5}{8}$
    D. $\frac{7}{10}$
    E. $\frac{5}{7}$

20. A student is entered in a college housing lottery for 2 consecutive years. Each year, 1 out of 5 students receives housing through the lottery. What is the probability that the student will receive housing through the lottery for at least 1 of these years?

    A. $\frac{1}{125}$
    B. $\frac{1}{5}$
    C. $\frac{9}{25}$
    D. $\frac{16}{25}$
    E. $\frac{4}{5}$

Combinations and Permutations

The number of possible arrangements of n different items is $n!$. If n is a positive integer, $n!$ is the product of the first n positive integers.

Example:

Beth, Tim, Sam, and Josh are going to stand in line. How many different ways can they line up?

The permutations formula, $_nP_k = \dfrac{n!}{(n-k)!}$, gives the number of **ordered** subgroups of k items that can be made from a set of n different items, where $k \leq n$.

Example:

Beth, Tim, Sam, Josh, Liz and Paul are eligible to be awarded first through fourth place in a cooking contest. How many different ways can first through fourth place be awarded?

The combinations formula, $_nC_k = \dfrac{n!}{k!(n-k)!}$, gives the number of **unordered** subgroups of k items that can be selected from a group of n different items, where $k \leq n$.

Example:

Beth, Tim, Sam, Josh, Liz and Paul are waiting for a bus. When the bus arrives, there is only room for 4 people to board. From this set of people, how many different groups of 4 can board the bus?

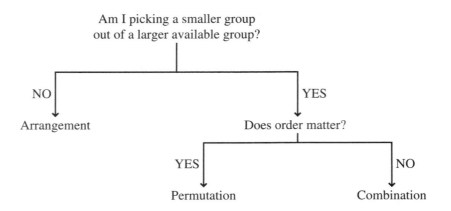

Example:

21. Amanda goes to the toy store to buy 1 ball and 3 different board games. If the toy store is stocked with 3 types of balls and 6 types of board games, how many different selections of the 4 items can Amanda make?

 A. 18
 B. 20 $n =$
 C. 24 $k =$
 D. 60
 E. 360

STUDY TIP

Memorize the definitions and equations for all of the terms in probability and statistics so you are fully prepared to solve these questions on Test Day.

Practice Questions

22.   Mike has 3 shirts, 2 ties, and 4 pairs of pants.

Quantity A	Quantity B
The number of non-identical complete outfits Mike can make	9

    A.   Quantity A is greater.
    B.   Quantity B is greater.
    C.   The two quantities are equal.
    D.   The relationship cannot be determined from the information given.

23. A lock requires a 4-digit code made from the numbers 0–9 without repetition of any of the numbers. How many different codes can be created?

    A.   210
    B.   3,024
    C.   5,040
    D.   6,561
    E.   10,000

24. Of the five distinct wires that lead into an apartment, two are for cable television and three are for telephone service. Using only these wires, how many distinct combinations of three wires are there such that at least one of the wires is for cable television?

    A.   3
    B.   6
    C.   7
    D.   8
    E.   9

Geometry and Trigonometry

Quadrilaterals and Circles

Rectangle

Area

$A = \text{length} \times \text{width} = l \times w$

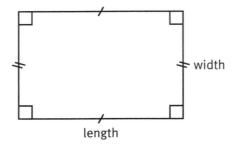

Perimeter

$P = 2l + 2w$

Square

Area

$A = \text{side} \times \text{side} = s^2$

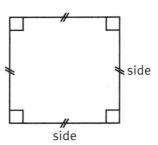

Perimeter

$P = 4s$

Trapezoid

Area

$A = \frac{1}{2}(\text{base}_1 + \text{base}_2) \times \text{height}$

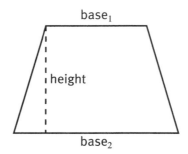

Example:

25. The figure below is made up of two squares and two rectangles. If the perimeter of square *RSZY* is 28 mm and the perimeter of square *ZUVW* is 16 mm, what is the sum of the areas of rectangles *STUZ* and *YZWX?*

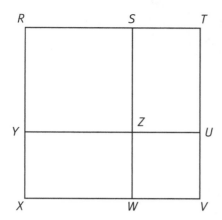

   A.   44 mm
   B.   56 mm
   C.   77 mm
   D.   105 mm
   E.   121 mm

Circles

Radius vs. Diameter

Area

$A = \pi r^2$

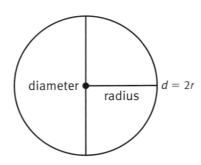

diameter • radius $d = 2r$

Circumference

$C = 2\pi r$

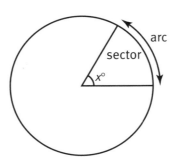

arc
sector
$x°$

Length of an Arc

$L_{arc} = \dfrac{X°}{360} \times C_{circle}$

Area of a Sector

$A_{sector} = \dfrac{X°}{360} \times A_{circle}$

Example:

26. What is the area of a 60° sector of a circle with a diameter of 6 cm?

    A. $\frac{3}{2}\pi$ cm^2

    B. 3π cm^2

    C. 6π cm^2

    D.   9 cm^2

    E. 9π cm^2

Practice Questions

27. A circle is inscribed in a square. If the area of the square is 144 meters, what is the area of the circle?

    A. 6π meters

    B. 12π meters

    C. 36π meters

    D. 48π meters

    E. 144π meters

28. The figure below represents four rectangles with the same center and lengths and widths as shown. If $x = 2$ and $y = 1$, what is the ratio of the smaller shaded area to the larger shaded area?

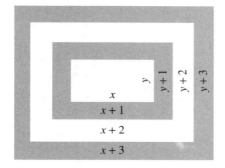

    A.   1:6

    B.   3:10

    C.   1:3

    D.   1:2

    E.   5:9

29.   A circle has area $9\pi\,\text{cm}^2$, and a square has area $9\,\text{cm}^2$.

              Quantity A   Quantity B

    The circumference of the circle   The perimeter of the square

    A.   Quantity A is greater.

    B.   Quantity B is greater.

    C.   The two quantities are equal.

    D.   The relationship cannot be determined from the information given.

Triangles

Area

$A = \frac{1}{2} bh$

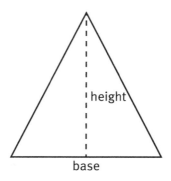 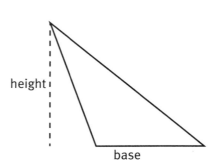

Perimeter

$P = a + b + c$

Pythagorean Theorem

$a^2 + b^2 = c^2$

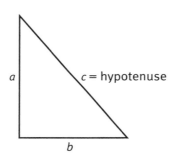

Special Right Triangles

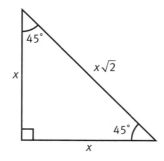 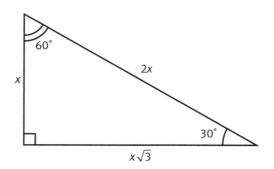

Pythagorean Triples

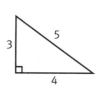 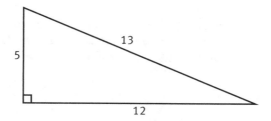

Other Pythagorean Triples:

7:24:25

8:15:17

9:40:41

Example:

30.   Joe and Conrad walk from Adelaide to Bel Air. Conrad walks directly to
        Bel Air, a distance of 5 miles. Joe walks due east for 3 miles and
        then walks due north until he reaches Bel Air.

<u>Quantity A</u>   <u>Quantity B</u>

4 miles   The distance Joe walks

- A.   Quantity A is greater.
- B.   Quantity B is greater.
- C.   The two quantities are equal.
- D.   The relationship cannot be determined from the information given.

Practice Questions

31. In the figure below, triangle *XYZ* has an area of 25 square feet and triangle *QRS* has an area of 100 square feet. If triangle *XYZ* and triangle *QRS* are similar, and line segment *QS* is 16 feet long, what is the length of line segment *XZ*?

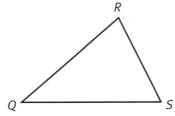
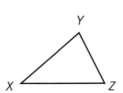

 A. 4 ft
 B. 5 ft
 C. $4\sqrt{2}$ ft
 D. $4\sqrt{3}$ ft
 E. 8 ft

32. If triangle *ABC* below is equilateral with side lengths of 4, and line segment *BD* is perpendicular to line segment *AC*, what is the length of line segment *BD*?

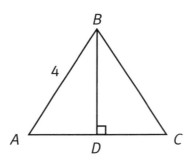

 A. 2
 B. $2\sqrt{2}$
 C. $2\sqrt{3}$
 D. 4
 E. $4\sqrt{3}$

Practice Questions

33. What is the area of the half circle in the figure shown below?

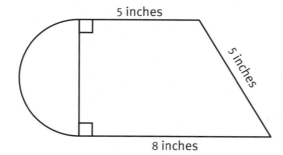

5 inches

5 inches

8 inches

A. 2π in^2

B. 4π in^2

C. 5π in^2

D. 8π in^2

E. 16π in^2

Trigonometry

Mnemonic: SOH-CAH-TOA

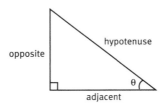

Numerical Values for Trigonometric Functions

o (degrees)	**0°**	**30°**	**45°**	**60°**	**90°**
π (radians)	**0 or 2π**	$\frac{\pi}{6}$	$\frac{\pi}{4}$	$\frac{\pi}{3}$	$\frac{\pi}{2}$
sin θ	$\frac{\sqrt{0}}{2}$	$\frac{\sqrt{1}}{2}$	$\frac{\sqrt{2}}{2}$	$\frac{\sqrt{3}}{2}$	$\frac{\sqrt{4}}{2}$
cos θ	$\frac{\sqrt{4}}{2}$	$\frac{\sqrt{3}}{2}$	$\frac{\sqrt{2}}{2}$	$\frac{\sqrt{1}}{2}$	$\frac{\sqrt{0}}{2}$

Sine

$$\sin \theta = \frac{\text{opposite}}{\text{hypotenuse}}$$

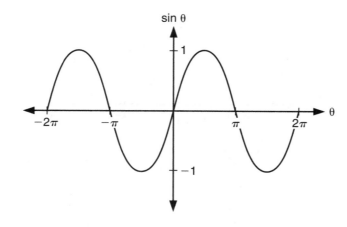

Domain: _____ Range: _____

x-intercepts: _____

Example:

34. Which of the following is equal to $2 \sin \left(\frac{\pi}{2}\right)$?

    A.   0

    B. $\sqrt{2}$

    C.   2

    D. π

    E. 2π

Cosine

$$\cos\theta = \frac{\text{adjacent}}{\text{hypotenuse}}$$

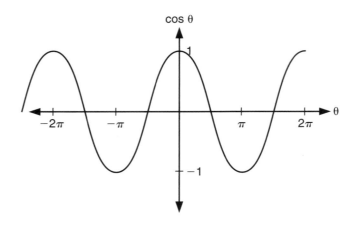

Domain: _____ Range: _____

x-intercepts: _____

Example:

35. Which of the following is equal to $11\cos\left(\frac{3\pi}{2}\right)$?

    A. 0

    B. $\frac{3}{2}$

    C. $\frac{3\pi}{2}$

    D. 11

    E. $\frac{33\pi}{2}$

Tangent

$$\tan \theta = \frac{\text{opposite}}{\text{adjacent}} = \frac{\sin \theta}{\cos \theta}$$

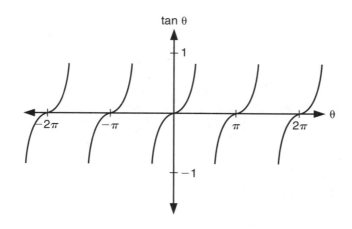

Domain: _____ Range: _____

x-intercepts: _____

Example

36. Which of the following is equal to 5 tan(0)?

    A.   0

    B.   1

    C.   π

    D.   5

    E.   5π

Practice Questions

37.

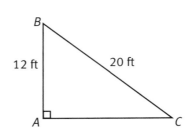

Quantity A

sine of angle ACB

Quantity B

cosine of angle ACB

A.   Quantity A is greater.
B.   Quantity B is greater.
C.   The two quantities are equal.
D.   The relationship cannot be determined from the information given.

38.   To determine the height h of a tree, Roger stands b feet from the base of the tree, as shown in the figure below, and measures the angle of elevation to be θ. Which of the following illustrates the relationship between h and b?

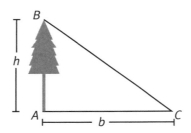

A. $\sin \theta = \dfrac{h}{b}$

B. $\sin \theta = \dfrac{b}{h}$

C. $\sin \theta = \dfrac{b}{\sqrt{b^2 + h^2}}$

D. $\sin \theta = \dfrac{h}{\sqrt{b^2 + h^2}}$

E. $\sin \theta = \dfrac{\sqrt{b^2 + h^2}}{b}$

39. In the figure below, if the length of line segment *CB* is *x*, what is the area of triangle *ABC* in terms of *x* and angle θ?

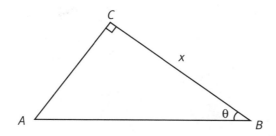

A. $\sin^2\theta + \cos^2\theta$

B. $\frac{1}{2} x^2 \tan \theta$

C. $\frac{1}{2} x^2 \sin \theta$

D. $\frac{1}{2} x^2 \cos \theta$

E. $x^2 \tan \theta$

Additional Trigonometric Functions

Inverse Trigonometric Functions	**Reciprocal Trigonometric Functions**

$\text{arcsin}(x) = \sin^{-1}(x)$

$\text{arccos}(x) = \cos^{-1}(x)$

$\text{arctan}(x) = \tan^{-1}(x)$

$\csc(x) = \dfrac{1}{\sin(x)}$

$\sec(x) = \dfrac{1}{\cos(x)}$

$\cot(x) = \dfrac{1}{\tan(x)}$

Example:

40. Which of the following is (or are) equivalent to $\cos^{-1}(1)$?

    A.   0

    B. $\dfrac{\sqrt{2}}{2}$

    C.   1

    D. π

    E.   Both (A) and (C)

STUDY TIP

Use your flashcards to memorize the important trigonometry relationships.

Practice Questions

41. Which of the following is equal to $-3\cos(\pi)$?

    A. -3
    B. -1
    C. 0
    D. 1
    E. 3

42.
Quantity A	Quantity B
$\sec(-\pi)$	$-\sec(\pi)$

    A.   Quantity A is greater.
    B.   Quantity B is greater.
    C.   The two quantities are equal.
    D.   The relationship cannot be determined from the information given.

43. A 6-foot ladder is propped against a wall so that the bottom of the ladder is 30 inches from the wall. What angle does the top of the ladder make with the wall?

    A. $\arccos\left(\frac{1}{5}\right)$

    B. $\arctan\left(\frac{12}{5}\right)$

    C. $\arcsin\left(\frac{5}{12}\right)$

    D. $\arccos\left(\frac{5}{12}\right)$

    E. $\arcsin\left(\frac{12}{5}\right)$

Study Plan

After Class: Quantitative Reasoning 2

Complete Remaining *Lesson Book* Practice Questions	30m	
Practice with Tests and Quizzes		

Before Class: General Chemistry 2

Read *Review Notes* Chapters 28–30, 34–37	4h 30m	

GENERAL CHEMISTRY 2

TOPICS COVERED

- Liquids and Solids
- Gases
- Solutions
- Acids and Bases
- Oxidation-Reduction Reactions
- Nuclear Reactions

After this session you will be able to:

- Calculate the energy involved in changing temperature and phase of matter
- Calculate the properties of gases using the ideal gas law
- Calculate the general and colligative properties of solutions
- Calculate pH and dissociation constant values for acids and bases
- Determine oxidizing and reducing numbers
- Calculate the energies associated with electrochemical cells
- Determine the products of radioactive decay

Liquids and Solids

Phases of Matter

Solid

Liquid

Gas

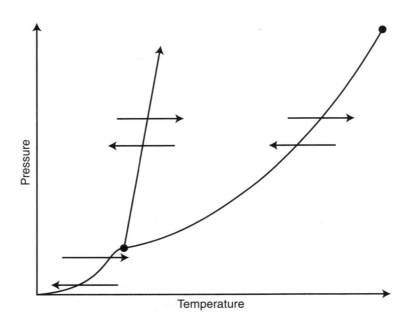

Critical Point

Triple Point

Practice Questions

1. The phase diagram for water looks different from most other phase diagrams in that its

    A.   critical point does not exist.
    B.   triple point is at 0 Pa.
    C.   phase is not dependent on pressure.
    D.   boundary line between solid and liquid phases has a negative slope.
    E.   boundary line between solid and liquid phases has a positive slope.

2. Which of the following processes is endothermic?

    A.   Condensation
    B.   Crystallization
    C.   Deposition
    D.   Freezing
    E.   Sublimation

3. When released in space, liquid water will first undergo vaporization but then quickly undergo deposition. What is the reason for this?

    A.   Solid ice has higher entropy than liquid water or gaseous water vapor, which is opposite of the enthalpy trend.
    B.   The low pressure in space allows the liquid to expand, but the low temperature leads to crystallization, which is the slower process.
    C.   The water vapor interacts with dark matter particles to form a new compound with a higher boiling point.
    D.   The energy within the water is converted into matter, which in turn releases energy.
    E.   Gases cannot exist long term in space, which means the majority of the material in space must be solid or liquid.

Phase Changes

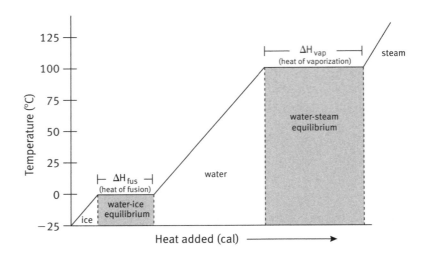

Specific Heat

Heat Capacity

$q = mc\Delta T$

Heat of Fusion

Heat of Vaporization

Vapor Pressure

TAKEAWAY

Be methodical with phase change calculations and make sure you don't miss any important pieces, whether heat capacity, heat of fusion, or heat of vaporization.

Practice Questions

4. Ice has a specific heat of 0.50 cal/g°C and a heat of fusion of 79.8 cal/g. How many calories are required to heat 12.0 g of water from –5°C to 25°C?

   A.   94.8 cal
   B.   107 cal
   C.   479 cal
   D.   1140 cal
   E.   1290 cal

5. What happens to the properties of a liquid when moved from sea level to higher altitudes?

   A.   Boiling point increases.
   B.   Boiling point decreases.
   C.   Vapor pressure increases.
   D.   Vapor pressure decreases.
   E.   Heat of vaporization increases.

6. A certain 10.0 g sample of paraffin wax has a heat capacity of 25 J/K. If the sample releases 575 J as it cools to 12.0°C, what was the original temperature?

   A.   2.30°C
   B.   9.70°C
   C.   14.3°C
   D.   23.0°C
   E.   35.0°C

Gases

Ideal Gases

Kinetic Molecular Theory of Gases

Temperature

Pressure

Mole Fraction (X)

$$X_A = \frac{\text{Moles of A}}{\text{Total moles of all components}}$$

Dalton's Law of Partial Pressures

$P_{total} = P_A + P_B + P_C + ...$

$P_A = X_A P_{total}$

Boyle's Law

$P_1 V_1 = P_2 V_2$

Charles's Law

$\dfrac{V_1}{T_1} = \dfrac{V_2}{T_2}$

Avogadro's Law

$\dfrac{V_1}{n_1} = \dfrac{V_2}{n_2}$

Ideal Gas Law

$PV = nRT$

STUDY TIP

Many of the gas laws are just restatements of the ideal gas law. If you understand the key relationships, you can answer any related questions on Test Day.

Practice Questions

7. What is the volume occupied by 3.2 g of oxygen at standard temperature and pressure?

    A.   2.24 L
    B.   4.48 L
    C.   22.4 L
    D.   32.0 L
    E.   44.8 L

8. A vessel contains 0.75 mol of nitrogen, 0.20 mol of hydrogen, and 0.05 mol of fluorine at a total pressure of 2.50 atm. What is the partial pressure of F_2?

    A.   0.050 atm
    B.   0.125 atm
    C.   0.50 atm
    D.   1.25 atm
    E.   2.50 atm

9. One mole of gas had its temperature changed to 546 K and its pressure increased to 3 atm. What is its new volume?

    A.   3.70 L
    B.   14.9 L
    C.   33.6 L
    D.   134 L
    E.   1,510 L

Solutions

Concentration Calculations

Solute

Solvent

Molarity (M)

$$M = \frac{\text{Moles of solute}}{\text{Liters of solutions}}$$

Molality (m)

$$m = \frac{\text{Moles of solute}}{\text{Kilograms of solvents}}$$

Dilution

$$M_1 V_1 = M_2 V_2$$

Practice Questions

10. Two hundred milliliters of water are added to 55 mL of a 7.5 M solution of KOH (56.1 g•mol^{-1}). What is the final concentration of the solution?

    A.   0.08 M
    B.   1.6 M
    C.   6.5 M
    D.   13 M
    E.   27 M

11. If 10 g of NaOH (40.0 g•mol^{-1}) are dissolved in 500 mL of water, what is the molality of the solution if the density of water is 1 g/mL?

    A.   0.005 m
    B.   0.5 m
    C.   0.6 m
    D.   0.8 m
    E.   20 m

12. Eighty grams of NaOH (40.0 g•mol^{-1}) are added to 195 mL of water. How much additional water is needed to make a final concentration of 5 M NaOH?

    A.   160 mL
    B.   205 mL
    C.   400 mL
    D.   410 mL
    E.   3810 mL

Colligative Properties

Vapor-Pressure Depression

$$\Delta P_{soln} = X_{solute} P_{solvent}^{\circ}$$

Boiling-Point Elevation

$$\Delta T_b = iK_b m$$

Freezing-Point Depression

$$\Delta T_f = iK_f m$$

$i =$ Van't hoff factor

$$\frac{Na^+ Cl^-}{= 2}$$

Osmotic Pressure

$$\Pi = iMRT$$

Solubility

Factors Affecting Solubility

AS temp ↑ solid Solid solubility ↑

AS temp ↑ gas solubility ↓

TAKEAWAY

Many solubility calculations rely on how many total moles of solute can be dissolved, so don't forget the van't Hoff factor for molecules that dissociate in solution.

Practice Questions

13. Which solute would lower the freezing point of 1 L of water the most if 2 moles of that solute were added?

    A.   NaCl

    B.   KCl

    C.   HCl

    D. H_2SO_4

    E. $C_6H_{12}O_6$

14. The K_b for water is 0.512°C•kg/mol. How much NaCl would need to be added to cause the boiling point of 4.0 L of water in a pot to rise by 1°C?

    A.   0.78 mol

    B.   2.0 mol

    C.   3.9 mol

    D.   7.8 mol

    E.   39 mol

15. A truck sprays a 20% by weight NaCl (58.5 g•mol^{-1}) solution on ice covering a road, causing the ice to melt. If water was used as the solvent when creating the solution, what is the freezing point of the solution given that the K_f of water is 1.9 K•kg•mol^{-1}?

    A.   −16°C

    B.   −13°C

    C.   −8.0°C

    D.   −4.3°C

    E.   −0.75°C

16. Maintaining the correct concentration of dissolved oxygen is important for aquatic life. Which change could cause an unsafe dip in oxygen levels within a fish tank?

    A.   Increasing water temperature

    B.   Decreasing water temperature

    C.   Dissolving less salt into the water

    D.   Increasing ambient pressure

    E.   Decreasing the number of fish present

Acids and Bases

Arrhenius /aqueous

Acid

Proton Donor

Base

OH⁻ Donor

Brønsted-Lowry

Acid

Proton Donor

Base

Proton acceptor

Lewis   Ligands/

Acid

electron pair acceptors (BF_3)

Base

Electron pair donors

(NH_3)

Conjugate Acids and Bases

$$CH_3COOH + H_2O \rightleftharpoons CH_3COO^- + H_3O^+$$

$$CH_3COO^- + H_2O \rightleftharpoons CH_3COOH + OH^-$$

Amphoteric Species

Autoionization of Water

$$H_2O \ (l) \rightleftharpoons H^+ \ (aq) + OH^- \ (aq)$$

$$K_w = [H^+][OH^-] = 1 \times 10^{-14}$$

Acid Dissociation Constant (K_a)

$$HA \ (aq) + H_2O \ (l) \rightleftharpoons A^- \ (aq) + H_3O^+ \ (aq)$$

$$K_a = \frac{[A^-][H_3O^+]}{[HA]}$$

Base Dissociation Constant (K_b)

$$B \ (aq) + H_2O \ (l) \rightleftharpoons HB^+ \ (aq) + OH^- \ (aq)$$

$$K_b = \frac{[HB^+][OH^-]}{[B]}$$

p Function

p(anything) = −log[anything]

Examples:

$pK_a = -\log(K_a)$

$pK_b = -\log(K_b)$

$pH = -\log[H^+]$

Strengths of Acids and Bases

Practice Questions

17. What is the pH of a solution at 25°C with a hydronium ion concentration of 6.4×10^{-3}?

    A.   1.7

    B.   2.2

    C.   3.6

    D.   4.0

    E.   6.4

18. The K_a of acetic acid (CH_3COOH) is 1.8×10^{-5} at 25°C. What is the K_b of acetate (CH_3COO^-) at 25°C?

    A. 3.6×10^{-19}

    B. 1.8×10^{-12}

    C. 5.6×10^{-10}

    D. 1.8×10^{-5}

    E. 1.8×10^{-2}

19. The pH of a specific acetic acid solution at standard conditions is 5.5. What is the pOH of that solution?

    A.   4.5

    B.   5.5

    C.   6.5

    D.   8.5

    E.   9.5

Practice Questions

20. What is the pH of a solution when 1.0×10^{-10} mol of HCl is added to 1 L of pure water?

    A. 3.6
    B. 5.9
    C. 7.0
    D. 9.9
    E. 10.0

21. The water autoionization reaction is endothermic. If the temperature is increased, what happens to the solution?

    A. The pH of the solution increases.
    B. The pH of the solution decreases.
    C. The pH of the solution stays the same.
    D. The solution becomes more acidic.
    E. The solution becomes more basic.

22. The relative permittivity of a solvent is a measure of its polarity; the higher its value, the better the solvent is at solvating ions. Below is a list of the relative permittivity of certain solvents at 20°C.

Solvent	Relative Permittivity
Hexane	1.9
Benzene	2.3
Diethyl ether	4.3
Methanol	30.0
Water	80.1

    If the same amount of nitric acid is added to 0.5 L of each solvent, which solvent would result in the solution with the highest pH?

    A. Hexane
    B. Benzene
    C. Diethyl ether
    D. Methanol
    E. Water

Titration

Equivalence Point

$$V_A N_A = V_B N_B$$

Normality

$$N = M \times \frac{\text{equivalents}}{\text{mol}}$$

$N = [c] \cdot (H/OH)$

\# of OH's or H+'s per mol

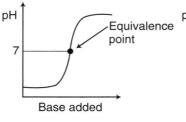

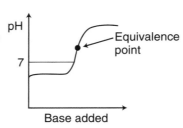

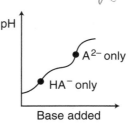

Buffers

Henderson-Hasselbalch Equation

$$pH = pK_a + \log \left[\frac{\text{conjugate base}}{\text{weak acid}} \right]$$

$$pOH = pK_b + \log \left[\frac{\text{conjugate acid}}{\text{weak base}} \right]$$

STUDY TIP

The DAT tests acids and bases using both calculation and conceptual questions. Memorizing formulas will help with calculations, but understanding relationships is essential for correctly answering conceptual questions.

Practice Questions

23. One hundred fifty milliliters of an unknown concentration of H_2SO_4 is found to reach equivalence after being titrated with 20 mL of a 2.0 M NaOH solution. What was the original H_2SO_4 concentration?

    A. 0.13 M
    B. 0.27 M
    C. 0.53 M
    D. 2.70 M
    E. 3.80 M

24. One liter of an aqueous ammonia ($K_b = 1.8 \times 10^{-5}$) solution is titrated with 1.1 N HCl (*aq*). If 50.0 mL of the acidic solution is required to reach the equivalence point, what was the pH of the ammonia solution before the titration was begun?

    A. 3.0
    B. 5.3
    C. 6.0
    D. 7.1
    E. 11.0

25. The pK_a of methyl red is 5.2. What is the ratio of acid to conjugate base of a 1 M solution of methyl red at pH 4.2?

red   yellow

    A. 10:1
    B. 7:1
    C. 1:1
    D. 1:9
    E. 1:10

Practice Questions

26. Which of the following chemicals would work best for determining the concentration of a formic acid solution via titration?

    A. Hydrochloric acid
    B. Ammonia
    C. Hydrogen sulfide
    D. Lithium hydroxide
    E. Acetone

27. To evaluate the endpoint of a titration of ammonia with a hydrobromic acid titrant, you should use the indicator

    A. methyl violet ($pK_{a2} = 1.8$).
    B. methyl orange ($pK_a = 3.7$).
    C. bromothymol blue ($pK_a = 7.0$).
    D. phenolphthalein ($pK_a = 9.3$).
    E. thymolphthalein ($pK_a = 9.9$).

28. Which of the following instruments would be most useful for measuring the amount of known base concentration added during the titration of 250 mL of an unknown acid?

    A. Pipette
    B. Burette
    C. Round-bottom flask
    D. Separatory funnel
    E. Retort

Oxidation-Reduction Reactions

Reduction

Oxidation

Reducing Agent

Oxidizing Agent

Oxidation Numbers

Rule 1: The oxidation number of free elements equals 0.

Rule 2: The oxidation number for a monoatomic ion equals its charge.

Rule 3: In a binary compound, the oxidation number of the more electronegative element equals its usual ionic charge.

Rule 4: The sum of the oxidation numbers of the atoms in a compound equals the overall charge of the compound.

Rule 5: Some elements usually have only one oxidation number.

Balancing Redox Equations

1. Separate the two half-reactions.

2. Balance the atoms, except H and O, of each separate half-reaction.

3. Use H_2O to balance the O atoms and then H^+ to balance the H atoms.

4. Use electrons to balance the charges of each half-reaction separately and then together such that each half-reaction has the same total number of electrons.

5. Combine the half-reactions, canceling out any molecules that appear on both sides of the equation.

6. In basic solution only: Add to both sides of the equation the same number of moles of OH^- as H^+ present, combine the H^+ and OH^- to make water, and cancel out any water molecules that appear on both sides of the equation.

7. Confirm that the numbers of atoms and charges are balanced.

Example: $MnO_4^- + AsO_3^{3-} \rightarrow MnO_2 + AsO_4^{3-}$

Practice Questions

29. What are the oxidizing and reducing agents in the following reaction?

$$AgNO_3 \ (aq) + CuNO_3 \ (aq) \rightarrow Ag \ (s) + Cu(NO_3)_2 \ (aq)$$

A. Cu is the oxidizing agent; Ag is the reducing agent.
B. Ag is the oxidizing agent; Cu is the reducing agent.
C. Ag is the oxidizing agent; NO_3 is the reducing agent.
D. NO_3 is the oxidizing agent; Cu is the reducing agent.
E. Cu is the oxidizing agent; NO_3 is the reducing agent.

30. What is the oxidation state of each nickel on the reactant side of the following reaction?

$$2 \ NiO(OH) + Cd + 2 \ H_2O \rightarrow 2 \ Ni(OH)_2 + Cd(OH)_2$$

A. -2
B. -1
C. 0
D. $+1$
E. $+3$

31. What is the complete and balanced reaction that involves the reagents indicated below?

$$MnO_4^- + C_2O_4^{2-} \rightarrow Mn^{2+} + CO_2$$

A. $16 \ H^+ + 5 \ C_2O_4^{2-} + 2 \ MnO_4^- \rightarrow 2 \ Mn^{2+} + 10 \ CO_2 + 8 \ H_2O$
B. $8 \ H^+ + 5 \ C_2O_4^{2-} + 2 \ MnO_4^- \rightarrow 2 \ Mn^{2+} + 10 \ CO_2 + 4 \ H_2O$
C. $16 \ H^+ + 5 \ C_2O_4^{2-} + 2 \ MnO_4^- \rightarrow 2 \ Mn^{2+} + 5 \ CO_2 + 8 \ H_2O$
D. $8 \ H^+ + 5 \ C_2O_4^{2-} + 2 \ MnO_4^- \rightarrow 2 \ Mn^{2+} + 5 \ CO_2 + 8 \ H_2O$
E. $8 \ H^+ + 5 \ C_2O_4^{2-} + 2 \ MnO_4^- \rightarrow 2 \ Mn^{2+} + 10 \ CO_2 + 8 \ H_2O$

Electrochemistry

Galvanic/Voltaic Cells

An OX Anode oxidadicn Cathode
Red Cat Reduction
Fat Cat
Anode → Cath

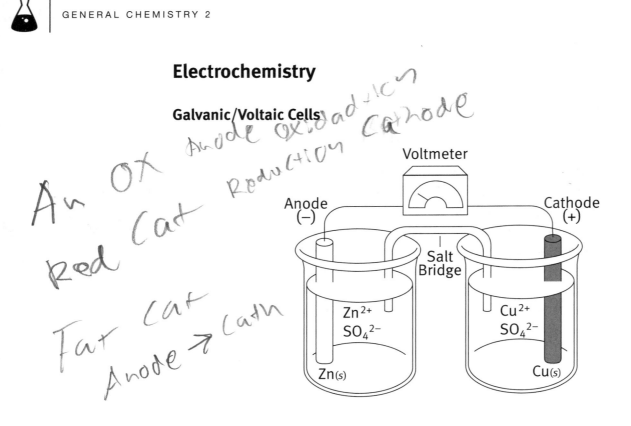

Electrolytic Cells

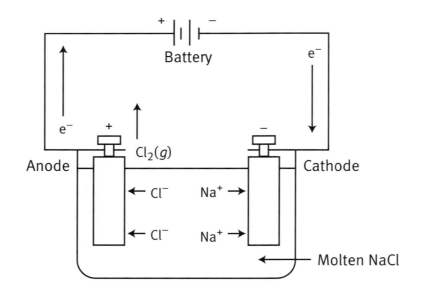

Reduction Potentials

Electromotive Force (emf)

$$E_{cell}^\circ = E_{cathode}^\circ - E_{anode}^\circ$$

Faraday's Laws of Electrolysis

$$It = nF$$

Gibbs Free Energy

$$\Delta G = -nFE_{cell}^\circ$$

$$\Delta G = -RT \ln K_{eq}$$

$$nFE_{cell}^\circ = RT \ln K_{eq}$$

STUDY TIP

Use your Quick Sheets to study the important equations you need to know for Test Day.

Practice Questions

Reaction	$E_{\text{reduction}}°$ (V)
$\text{ZnS}\ (s) + 2\ e^- \rightarrow \text{Zn}\ (s) + \text{S}^{2-}\ (aq)$	-1.440
$\text{Zn}^{2+}\ (aq) + 2\ e^- \rightarrow \text{Zn}\ (s)$	-0.763
$\text{Cu}^{2+}\ (aq) + 2\ e^- \rightarrow \text{Cu}\ (s)$	$+0.337$

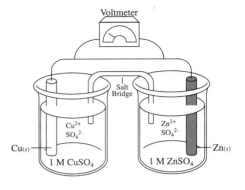

32. The cell above is an example of

    A.   a galvanic cell with a zinc cathode and a copper anode.

    B.   an electrolytic cell with a zinc cathode and a copper anode.

    C.   a galvanic cell with a zinc anode and a copper cathode.

    D.   an electrolytic cell with a zinc anode and a copper cathode.

    E.   a galvanic cell with a zinc anode and a sulfur cathode.

33. What is the standard cell potential of the above cell?

    A. -1.10 V

    B. -0.430 V

    C. $+0.430$ V

    D. 1.10 V

    E. 1.78 V

34. If the following reaction produces a current of 3 A for 2.0 seconds, how many moles of Na (s) are consumed?

$$\text{CO}^{3+}\ (aq) + \text{Na}\ (s) \rightarrow \text{CO}^{2+}\ (aq) + \text{Na}^+\ (aq)$$

    A. 6.0×10^{-5}

    B. 6.0×10^{-4}

    C. 1.5×10^{-4}

    D. 1.5×10^4

    E. 6.0×10^5

Nuclear Reactions

Alpha Decay (α)

$$^{A}_{Z}X \rightarrow \,^{A-4}_{Z-2}Y + \alpha$$

Beta Minus Decay (β^-): Electron Emission

$$^{A}_{Z}X \rightarrow \,^{A}_{Z+1}Y + e^{-}$$

Electron Capture

$$^{A}_{Z}X + e^{-} \rightarrow \,^{A}_{Z-1}Y$$

Beta Plus Decay (β^+): Positron Emission

$$^{A}_{Z}X \rightarrow \,^{A}_{Z-1}Y + e^{+}$$

Gamma Decay (γ)

$$^{A}_{Z}X^{*} \rightarrow \,^{A}_{Z}X + \gamma$$

Half-Life ($t_{1/2}$)

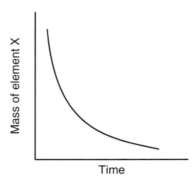

Time elapsed	Sample remaining
0 half-life	100%
1 half-life	50%
2 half-lives	25%
3 half-lives	12.5%

Fraction remaining after n half-lives $= \left(\frac{1}{2}\right)^{n}$

Fraction of nuclei decayed after n half-lives $= 1 - \left(\frac{1}{2}\right)^{n}$

STUDY TIP

In-depth knowledge of quantum physics isn't necessary for Test Day. Memorize the effects of each nuclear reaction so you can move on to study higher-yield topics.

Practice Questions

35. Uranium-238 ($Z = 92$) can undergo a single alpha decay to form a daughter with a mass number of

    A. 234.
    B. 236.
    C. 238.
    D. 240.
    E. 242.

36. Plutonium-241 ($Z = 94$) can transform into americium-241 ($Z = 95$). This is an example of

    A. alpha decay.
    B. beta minus decay.
    C. beta plus decay.
    D. electron capture.
    E. gamma decay.

37. After 82 days, $\frac{15}{16}$ of a sample of einsteinium-253 has decayed. What is the $t_{\frac{1}{2}}$ of einsteinium-253?

    A. 4.0 days
    B. 5.1 days
    C. 20.5 days
    D. 27.3 days
    E. 328 days

Study Plan

After Class: General Chemistry 2

Complete Remaining *Lesson Book* Practice Questions	30m	
Practice with Tests and Quizzes		

Before Class: Organic Chemistry 2

Read *Review Notes* Chapters 44–51	3h 0m	

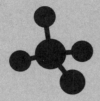

ORGANIC CHEMISTRY 2

TOPICS COVERED

- Aromatics and Bonding
- Reactions
- Acid-Base Chemistry
- Properties of Molecules and Organic Analysis

After this session you will be able to:

- Determine aromaticity
- Describe the properties of and predict the products of reactions involving aromatics, alcohols, ethers, carbonyls, and carboxylic acid derivatives
- Identify specific named chemical reactions
- Determine the relative strengths of acids and bases
- Interpret results from IR and NMR spectroscopy
- Evaluate the separation methods of extraction and distillation

Aromatics and Bonding

Bond Types

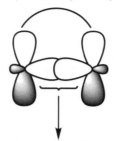

side-to-side overlap of
two p orbitals (π bond)

end-to-end overlap of
2 hybridized orbitals
(σ bond)

Sigma (σ)

Pi (π)

Hybridization

Hybridization	# of σ bonds	Bond angle
sp^3		
sp^2		
sp		

Conjugation

α, β-unsaturated carbonyl

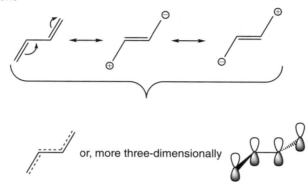

1, 3 diene

or, more three-dimensionally

Aromaticity

Practice Questions

$$H-C\equiv C-C-H$$

1. How many sigma bonds are in the above molecule?

    A.   4
    B.   7
    C.   8
    D.   10
    E.   13

2. How many pi bonds are in the above molecule?

    A.   1
    B.   2
    C.   3
    D.   4
    E.   5

3. What is the angle between any two of the hydrogens in ammonia, NH_3?

    A.   104.5°
    B.   107°
    C.   109.5°
    D.   120°
    E.   180°

Practice Questions

4. What is the hybridization of the two carbons in ethene, C_2H_4?

    A. sp^0 (none)

    B. sp

    C. sp^2

    D. sp^3

    E.   Both sp^2 and sp^3

5. Is the following compound aromatic?

    A.   Yes, because the compound is conjugated.

    B.   Yes, because the compound is cyclic.

    C.   Yes, because the molecule emits a pleasant odor.

    D.   No, because the compound has six pi electrons.

    E.   No, because the molecule violates Hückel's rule.

6. Which of the following compounds is aromatic?

    I.

    II.

    III.

    A.   II

    B.   III

    C.   II and III

    D.   I, II, and III

    E.   None of the above

Electrophilic Aromatic Substitution

General Mechanism

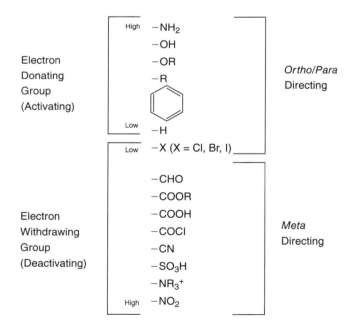

Substituent Effects in EAS Reactions

Activators vs. Deactivators

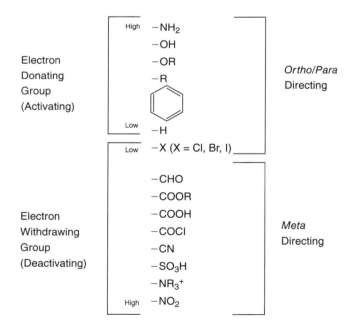

STUDY TIP

Although you won't have many questions directly related to EAS, understanding electron-withdrawing and electron-donating groups will help you earn many points on questions about various other reactions.

Practice Questions

7. A chemist used electrophilic aromatic substitution in order to complete the following reaction. In what order must the substituents have been added?

A. The nitro group was added first, then the alcohol group was added.
B. The alcohol group was added first, then the nitro group was added.
C. Both were added at the same time in the presence of heat.
D. The order in which the groups were added does not matter.
E. One group was added at a time, but the order cannot be determined.

8. What will be the product(s) of the following reaction?

HNO_3/H_2SO_4

A.

B.

C. and

D.

E. and

9. Each of the following is an electron-donating group EXCEPT one. Which one is the EXCEPTION?

A. OH
B. CH_3
C. NH_2
D. C_6H_6
E. Cl

Reactions

Alcohols and Ethers

$$R-OH \qquad R-O-R'$$

Nomenclature

Electrophile

Nucleophile

Leaving Group

$$R-OH \xrightarrow{\ H^+\ } R-OH_2$$

Acidity

$$R-OH \longrightarrow R-O^- + H^+$$

Alcohol Synthesis

Alkene + H_2O → Alcohol

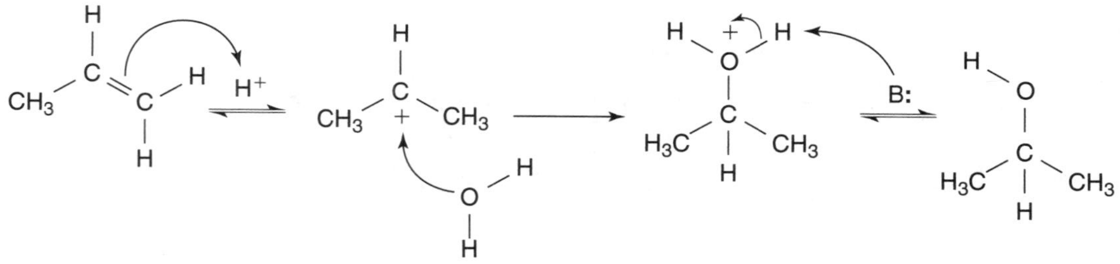

Ether Synthesis

2 Alcohol → Ether + Water

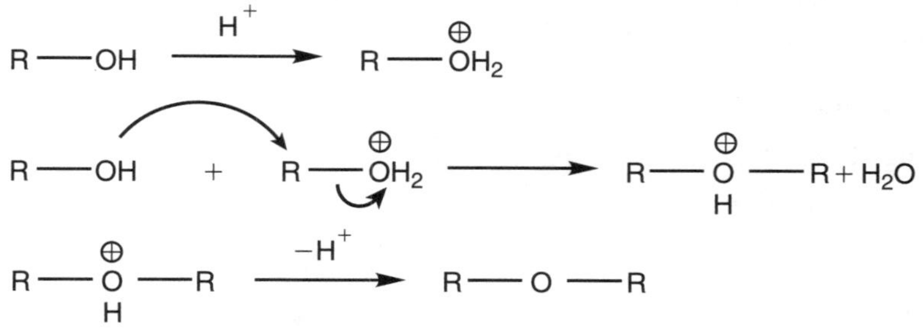

Williamson Ether Synthesis

Alcohol + Alkyl Halide → Ether + Salt

Practice Questions

10. Treatment of diisopropyl ether with two equivalents of hydrogen bromide (below) yields what product(s)?

$$CH_3-\overset{\overset{\displaystyle CH_3}{|}}{CH}-O-\overset{\overset{\displaystyle CH_3}{|}}{CH}-CH_3 \ + 2\,HBr \longrightarrow$$

    A.   1-Bromopropane

    B.   1-Bromopentane

    C.   2-Bromopropane

    D.   2-Bromopropanol

    E.   1-Bromopropane and 1-propanol

11. Ethene can be reacted with steam to form ethanol via a hydration reaction; yields from this reaction are low but can be improved by

    A.   adding base.

    B.   adding H_2 and Pd.

    C.   removing water.

    D.   removing heat.

    E.   removing ethanol product.

12. Why do alcohols generally have higher boiling points than ethers?

    A.   Ethers are more polar than alcohols.

    B.   Alcohols have hydrogen bonding but ethers do not.

    C.   Ethers have lower atomic weights than alcohols.

    D.   Ethers cannot form ions.

    E.   Alcohols have more branching in their side chains.

Carbonyls: Aldehydes and Ketones

$$R-\overset{\overset{\displaystyle O}{\|}}{C}-H \qquad R-\overset{\overset{\displaystyle O}{\|}}{C}-R'$$

Nomenclature

Electrophile

Nucleophile

$$R-\overset{\overset{\displaystyle O}{\|}}{C}-R' \xrightarrow{\;H^+\;} R-\overset{\overset{\displaystyle \overset{\oplus}{O}H}{\|}}{C}-R' \longleftrightarrow R-\overset{\overset{\displaystyle OH}{|}}{\underset{\oplus}{C}}-R'$$

Carbonyl Synthesis

Alkyne + H_2O → Carbonyl

General Carbonyl Reactions

Acidity and Alpha Hydrogen

keto form ⇌ enol form

Keto-Enol Tautomerism

Aldol Reactions

Aldol Addition

ketone enolate + aldehyde ⟶ aldol

Aldol Condensation

Practice Questions

13. What is the product of the following reaction?

+ NaCN ⟶

A. 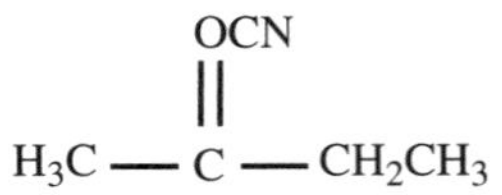
$$H_3C - \underset{\overset{\parallel}{OCN}}{C} - CH_2CH_3$$

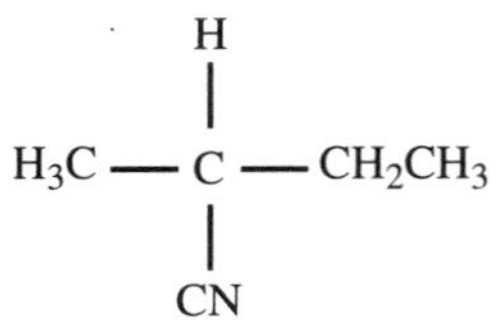

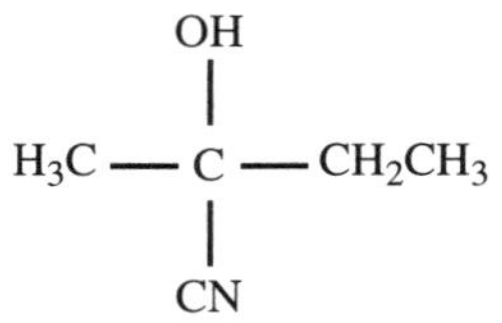

D. 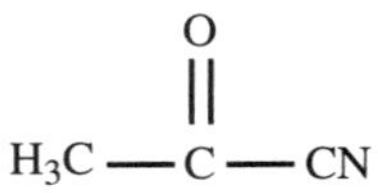
$$H_3C - \underset{\overset{\parallel}{O}}{C} - CN$$

B.
$$H_3C - \underset{\underset{CN}{|}}{\overset{\overset{H}{|}}{C}} - CH_2CH_3$$

E. 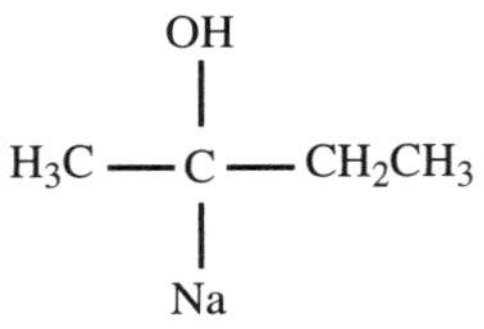
$$H_3C - \underset{\underset{Na}{|}}{\overset{\overset{OH}{|}}{C}} - CH_2CH_3$$

C.
$$H_3C - \underset{\underset{CN}{|}}{\overset{\overset{OH}{|}}{C}} - CH_2CH_3$$

14. Which of the following reactions produces the compound below?

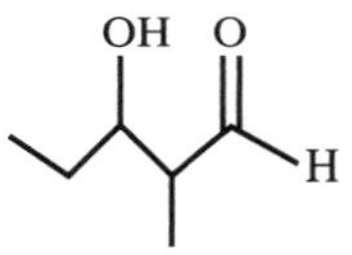

A. $CH_3CHO + CH_3CH_2CH_2CHO \rightarrow$
B. $CH_3COCH_3 + CH_3CH_2CH_2CHO \rightarrow$
C. $CH_3CH_2COCH_3 + CH_3CHO \rightarrow$
D. $CH_3CH_2CHO + CH_3CH_2CHO \rightarrow$
E. $CH_3CHO + CH_3COCH_3 \rightarrow$

15. Which hydrogen atom in the compound below is the most acidic?

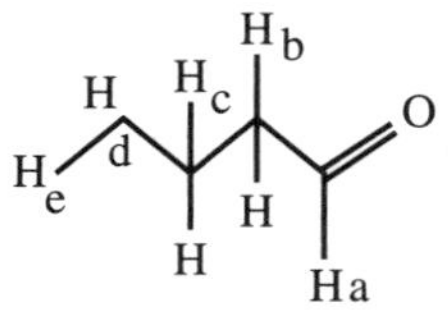

A. a
B. b
C. c
D. d
E. e

Carbonyls: Carboxylic Acids

$$O=\!\!\!\overset{OH}{\underset{R}{C}} \longrightarrow \left[O=\!\!\!\overset{O^-}{\underset{R}{C}} \longleftrightarrow \overset{O^-}{\underset{R}{C}}\!\!\!=O \right] + \ H^+$$

Nomenclature

Electrophile

Nucleophile

Leaving Group

Acidity

Carboxylic Acid Synthesis

Amide/Ester + Water → Carboxylic Acid

$$R_1\!\!-\!\!C(=O)\!\!-\!\!NH\!\!-\!\!R_2 \xrightarrow{H_2O} R_1\!\!-\!\!C(=O)\!\!-\!\!OH \ + \ H_2N\!\!-\!\!R_2$$

$$R_1\!\!-\!\!C(=O)\!\!-\!\!OR_2 \xrightarrow{H_2O} R_1\!\!-\!\!C(=O)\!\!-\!\!O^\ominus \ + \ R_2OH$$

Carbonyls: Carboxylic Acid Derivatives

Reactivity

most reactive

least reactive

General Substitution Reaction

Carboxylic Acid + Nucleophile → Carboxylic Acid Derivative

Acyl Halide Formation

Carboxylic Acid + Thionyl Chloride → Acyl Chloride

Ester Formation

Carboxylic Acid + Alcohol → Ester

Practice Questions

16. What type of reaction is represented below?

triacylglyceride + HOH → fatty acid + diacylglyceride

    A.   Hydration
    B.   Hydrolysis
    C.   Hydrogenation
    D.   Dehydration
    E.   Esterification

17. Which of the following will undergo ester hydrolysis most rapidly?

18. Why should esterification reactions not be carried out in water?

    A.   Acid is insoluble in water.
    B.   The polar nature of water overshadows the polar nature of the carboxyl group.
    C.   The extensive hydrogen bonding of water interferes with the S_N2 reaction mechanism.
    D.   Water molecules would hydrolyze useful products back to the parent carboxylic acid.
    E.   Water would cause the carboxylic acid to ionize, so no reaction would occur.

Named Reactions

Grignard Reaction

Carbonyl + Grignard Reagent → Alcohol

Diels-Alder Reaction

Diene + Dienophile → Ring

Wittig Alkene Synthesis

Aldehyde/Ketone + Triphenyl Phosphonium Ylide → Alkene

$$\underset{R_2}{\overset{R_1}{>}}C=O \;+\; \underset{R_4}{\overset{Ph_3-P^+}{>}}C^- -R_3 \longrightarrow \underset{R_2}{\overset{R_1}{>}}C=C\underset{R_4}{\overset{R_3}{<}} \;+\; Ph_3P=O$$

Practice Questions

19. What is the product of the following reaction?

   A. 1-Phenyl-1-butanol
   B. 1-Phenyl-2-butanol
   C. 1-Methyl-1-phenyl-1-propanol
   D. 2-Phenyl-2-butanol
   E. 2-Phenyl-2-pentanol

20. Why must a diene be able to exist in the *cis* conformation to undergo the Diels-Alder reaction?

   A. The energy of the products is lower than that of the reactants when using the *trans* conformation.
   B. The *trans* conformations of dienes have too many electron-donating groups.
   C. The double bonds in the *trans* conformation are too close together to allow reaction.
   D. Only the *cis* conformation shows conjugation, which is required for the reaction to proceed.
   E. If the *trans* conformation is too sterically hindered to rotate about the bond, a ring cannot form.

21. Which of the following most accurately describes the mechanism of the Wittig reaction?

   A. The first step is nucleophilic attack on the carbonyl carbon.
   B. The electrophile is the anionic carbon of the ylide.
   C. Phosphorous bonds with oxygen to stabilize the alkene final product.
   D. The mechanism can only proceed if the ylide reacts with a ketone.
   E. The final step of the mechanism is hydrolysis of the four-membered oxaphosphetane ring.

Oxidation-Reduction Reactions

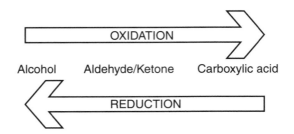

Reducing Agents

Oxidizing Agents

General Oxidation Reactions

Primary Alcohols

$$\text{H}_3\text{C}-\overset{\overset{\displaystyle \text{OH}}{|}}{\underset{\underset{\displaystyle \text{H}}{|}}{\text{C}}}-\text{H} \xrightarrow{\text{PCC}} \text{H}_3\text{C}-\overset{\displaystyle \text{O}}{\text{C}}-\text{H} \xrightarrow[\text{Reagent}]{\text{Tollens'}} \text{H}_3\text{C}-\overset{\displaystyle \text{O}}{\text{C}}-\text{OH}$$

$$\text{KMnO}_4, \text{K}_2\text{Cr}_2\text{O}_7, \text{etc.}$$

Secondary Alcohols

$$\text{H}_3\text{C}-\overset{\overset{\displaystyle \text{OH}}{|}}{\text{C}}-\text{CH}_3 \longrightarrow \text{H}_3\text{C}-\overset{\displaystyle \text{O}}{\text{C}}-\text{CH}_3$$

Tertiary Alcohols

$$\text{H}_3\text{C}-\overset{\overset{\displaystyle \text{OH}}{|}}{\underset{\underset{\displaystyle \text{CH}_3}{|}}{\text{C}}}-\text{CH}_3 \not\longrightarrow \text{H}_3\text{C}-\overset{\displaystyle \text{O}}{\underset{\underset{\displaystyle \text{CH}_3}{|}}{\text{C}}}\begin{matrix}\text{CH}_3 \\ \text{CH}_3\end{matrix}$$

Oxidative Cleavage of Alkenes

Alkene + Oxidizing Agent → 2 Carbonyls

non-terminal alkene

1) $KMnO_4$, OH^-, heat
2) H^+

→ 2 (carboxylic acid)

terminal alkene

1) $KMnO_4$, OH^-, heat
2) H^+

→ (carboxylic acid) $+CO_2$

non-terminal alkene

1) O_3, CH_2Cl_2
2) Zn/H_2O

→ 2 (aldehyde)

General Reduction Reactions

Aldehyde →

Ketone →

Ester →

Carboxylic Acid →

NaBH$_4$

LiAlH$_4$

Practice Questions

22. What is the product of the following reaction?

$$(CH_3)_2CHCH_2OH \xrightarrow{\text{KMnO}_4}$$

    A.   2-Methylethanal

    B.   2-Methylpropanal

    C.   2-Methylpropanoic acid

    D.   Butanal

    E.   Butanoic acid

23. Upon ozonolysis of an unknown alkene, the following two compounds were formed.

$$\underset{CHCH_2CH_3}{\overset{O}{\underset{\|}{\|}}} \quad \text{and} \quad \underset{CH_3CCH_3}{\overset{O}{\underset{\|}{\|}}}$$

What was the original alkene?

    A.   2-Methyl-2-butene

    B.   2-Methyl-2-pentene

    C.   2-Methyl-2-hexene

    D.   3-Methyl-2-pentene

    E.   3-Methyl-2-hexene

24. Which of the following would NOT react in the presence of $NaBH_4$?

    A.   Cyclohexanone

    B.   Ethyl ethanoate

    C.   Formaldehyde

    D.   Propanal

    E.   All of the above would react in the presence of $NaBH_4$.

Acid-Base Chemistry

Determining Acid Strength

Resonance Effects

Induction: Electron-Withdrawing Groups

(1) The closer the electron-withdrawing group to the acidic hydrogen, the stronger the acid.

more stable than

(2) The more electronegative the electron-withdrawing group, the stronger the acid.

more stable than

(3) The larger the number of electron-withdrawing groups, the stronger the acid.

more stable than

Hybridization

$$R-C\equiv C-H \longrightarrow R-C\equiv C{:}^{\ominus}$$ $pK_a \approx 22$

$$\underset{H}{\overset{R}{>}}C=C\underset{H}{\overset{H}{<}} \longrightarrow \underset{H}{\overset{R}{>}}C=C\underset{H}{\overset{\ominus}{<}}$$ $pK_a \approx 40$

$$R-\underset{H}{\overset{H}{\underset{|}{C}}}-\underset{H}{\overset{H}{\underset{|}{C}}}-H \longrightarrow R-\underset{H}{\overset{H}{\underset{|}{C}}}-\underset{H}{\overset{H}{\underset{|}{C}}}{:}^{\ominus}$$ $pK_a \approx 60$

Determining Base Strength

Resonance Effects

Induction: Electron-Donating Groups

Hybridization and Non-Bonded Electron Pairs

STUDY TIP

Acids and bases are tested in both the General Chemistry and the Organic Chemistry sections of the Survey of the Natural Sciences. Study all of this content together to help you make better connections and earn more points for your effort.

Practice Questions

25. Which represents the order of increasing basicity for the following compounds?

I.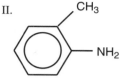

II.

III.

A.   I < II < III
B.   II < III < I
C.   II < I < III
D.   III < I < II
E.   III < II < I

26. Which represents the order of increasing acidity for the following compounds?

I.

III.

II.

IV.

A.   I < II < III < IV
B.   I < II < IV < III
C.   II < I < III < IV
D.   II < I < IV < III
E.   IV < III < II < I

Properties of Molecules and Organic Analysis

Spectroscopy

IR

Practice Questions

27. A student attempting to determine the identity of an unknown sample employs IR spectroscopy to analyze it and obtains the following spectrum:

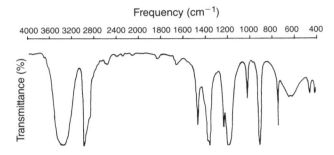

Based on the spectrum, the identity of the unknown compound is most likely to be

    A.   butanamine.

    B.   benzaldehyde.

    C.   hexane.

    D.   propanol.

    E.   pentanone.

28. A chemist performs an organic synthesis that requires the oxidation of *sec*-butanol to 2-butanone. Based on the following IR spectrum, which of the following would provide the best evidence that he successfully completed this conversion?

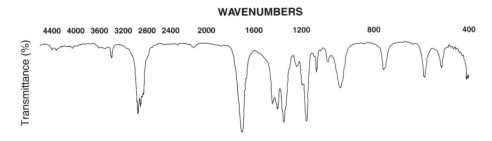

    A.   Noting the appearance of a broad absorption peak in the region of 1000–800 cm^{-1}

    B.   Noting the appearance of a strong absorption peak in the region of 1700 cm^{-1}

    C.   Noting the appearance of two sharp peaks at 3000 cm^{-1}

    D.   Noting the appearance of multiple peaks in the fingerprint region

    E.   Noting the appearance of a broad absorption peak in the region of 1900–2700 cm^{-1}

Nuclear Magnetic Resonance (NMR)

^{1}H NMR

Practice Questions

29. Which of the following compounds will produce the given ^{1}H NMR spectrum?

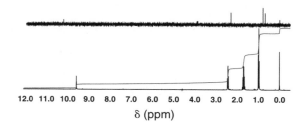

A. 2-Chloropentane
B. Butanal
C. Benzoic acid
D. Methanal
E. 2-Pentene

30. Which of the following compounds will produce the given ^{1}H NMR spectrum?

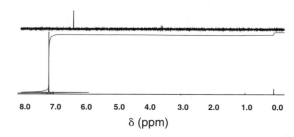

A. Benzene
B. Benzoic acid
C. Acetone
D. Methane
E. Octene

^{13}C NMR

Practice Questions

31. How many peaks would you expect to see on a ^{13}C NMR spectrum of toluene, shown below?

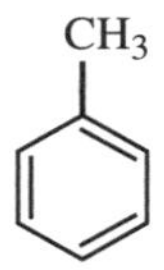

CH$_3$

toluene

    A.   1

    B.   3

    C.   5

    D.   7

    E.   9

32. Which of the following spectra most likely corresponds to alanine, shown below?

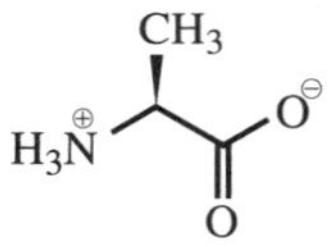

CH$_3$

H$_3$N$^{\oplus}$ O$^{\ominus}$

O

alanine

    A.   168.10 ppm, 159.91 ppm, 144.05 ppm, 95.79 ppm

    B.   207.85 ppm, 172.69 ppm, 29.29 ppm

    C.   178.54 ppm, 53.25 ppm, 18.95 ppm

    D.   183.81 ppm, 182. 63 ppm, 73.06 ppm, 45.35 ppm

    E.   167.9 ppm, 136.5 ppm, 125.4 ppm, 51.8 ppm, 18.4 ppm

Practice Questions

33. A chemist observes a broad IR stretch at 3,400 cm^{-1}. Which of the following groups is being observed?

    A. C=O
    B. N–H
    C. O–H
    D. C=C
    E. C–H

34. How many peaks would you expect to see on a proton NMR spectrum of (*E*)-buten-2-ol?

    A. 0
    B. 1
    C. 2
    D. 3
    E. 4

35. A proton is one bond away from a methyl group in which all protons are equivalent. What is the splitting pattern seen on the first proton?

    A. Singlet
    B. Doublet
    C. Triplet
    D. Quadruplet
    E. No splitting is seen.

Separation

Extraction

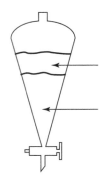

Aqueous Layer

Organic Layer

Intermolecular Forces

Using Acids and Bases

Distillation

Simple

Fractional

Vacuum

> **STUDY TIP**
> The DAT does not expect you to be an organic lab expert. Memorize
> the key values for spectroscopy, but otherwise focus on the concepts
> behind how lab techniques work rather than every specific detail.

Practice Questions

36. A chemist plans to purify a mixture of two liquids by using distillation followed by recrystallization. What must be true of the two liquids in order for this technique to be successful?

    A. The liquids must have different solubilities.
    B. The liquids must have different molecular weights.
    C. The liquids must have different densities.
    D. The liquids must have different precipitates.
    E. The liquids must have different boiling points.

37. At the end of an experiment, a solution of benzoic acid is contaminated with cresol. A student attempts to isolate benzoic acid by carrying out two extraction experiments. Part of the mixture is extracted using NaOH and the other part is extracted using $NaHCO_3$. Spectroscopic data shows that the extraction was more successful using $NaHCO_3$. Why would these results be observed?

    A. $NaHCO_3$ is a weak base and only deprotonates cresol, whereas NaOH protonates both cresol and benzoic acid.
    B. $NaHCO_3$ is a weak base and only deprotonates benzoic acid, whereas NaOH reacts with both cresol and benzoic acid.
    C. $NaHCO_3$ is a weak base and only protonates cresol, whereas NaOH protonates both cresol and benzoic acid.
    D. $NaHCO_3$ is a strong base and protonates both benzoic acid and cresol, but NaOH only reacts with benzoic acid.
    E. $NaHCO_3$ is a strong base and only protonates benzoic acid, whereas NaOH reacts with both cresol and benzoic acid.

38. An alcohol distillery wants to obtain 100% ethanol. They currently have an azeotropic mixture of 95% ethanol, which means that the ethanol and water boil at the same temperature. What technique should be used to separate this mixture?

    A. Simple distillation
    B. Fractional distillation
    C. Vacuum distillation
    D. Recrystallization
    E. It is impossible to separate an azeotropic mixture.

Study Plan

After Class: Organic Chemistry 2

Complete Remaining *Lesson Book* Practice Questions	30m	
Practice with Tests and Quizzes		

Before Class: Reading Comprehension 2

Read *Review Notes* Chapter 54	60m	

READING COMPREHENSION 2

TOPICS COVERED

- Kaplan Reading Comprehension Strategy Review
- Running Out of Time Strategy

After this session you will be able to:

- Apply the strategies you have already learned to any question on your exam

Kaplan Reading Comprehension Strategy Review

READ STRATEGICALLY

→ Preview the passage for Topic
→ Anticipate while reading using Keywords
→ Map each paragraph's Scope
→ Determine the author's Tone
→ Identify the author's overall Purpose

The Kaplan Question Strategy

STOP

→ Characterize the question type.

THINK

→ What is the question really asking?
→ Where is the relevant information you need?

PREDICT

→ Formulate a framework or prediction for your answer.

MATCH

→ Select the answer that truly meets the requirements of the prediction.

Question Types

Type	Task
Global	
Detail	
Detail EXCEPT	
Function	
Inference	
Other	

Identify the question type for the following question stems:

1. According to the passage, the goal of Flowers's experiment was to

2. The author mentions excavations at Susa in order to

3. Which of the following most accurately describes the passage?

4. Which of the following would most weaken Janis's hypothesis?

5. Each of the following is listed as an example of a difference between the giant panda and a typical bear EXCEPT one. Which is the EXCEPTION?

6. It can be inferred from the passage that some researchers believe that the site discovered in the Yucatan

a. Global

b. Detail

c. Detail EXCEPT

d. Function

e. Inference

f. Other

Kaplan Answer Choice Strategy

Wrong Answer Choice Pathologies

Pathology	Why it's wrong	Why it's seductive
Faulty Use of Detail		
Opposite		
Distortion		
Out of Scope		

Passage 1

Mapping Exercise

Heart Disease

(1). Today, there is a fairly standard model of the factors leading to heart disease. Most heart disease is caused by the growth of fatty deposits, known as atherosclerotic plaques, in coronary artery walls. Plaques narrow the width of arteries and also lead to the formation of clots that can block the flow of blood, eventually causing a heart attack. Factors such as high blood pressure, smoking, and diabetes increase the risk of heart disease. High levels of cholesterol and saturated fats in the diet also increase the risk because they contribute to plaque formation.

(2). A sizable minority of coronary patients, however, experience heart attacks even though they display few or no standard risk factors. Recent research by Richard M. Lawn suggests that lipoprotein(a), a blood protein first isolated in the 1960s, may play a major role in such cases. Excessive levels of lipoprotein(a) are associated with strokes, heart attacks, and the narrowing of coronary arteries. In fact, males with high lipoprotein(a) levels account for about one quarter of male heart attack victims under the age of 60.

(3). Lipoprotein(a) is closely related to low-density lipoprotein (LDL), a major contributor to atherosclerosis. As a group, lipoproteins absorb and transport fatty substances, including cholesterol, to various sites in the body. High-density lipoproteins, or HDLs, are protective and carry cholesterol to the liver for later use in the synthesis of important hormones; LDLs, however, deposit cholesterol in the bloodstream, including in coronary arteries, where it contributes to plaque formation. Lipoprotein(a) has almost the same complex structure as LDL, with an additional surface protein called apolipoprotein(a). Apolipoprotein(a) resembles plasminogen, a protein that binds with and dissolves fibrin, a key component of blood clots. Unlike plasminogen, however, apolipoprotein(a) does not dissolve fibrin.

(4). A theory that would adequately explain how lipoprotein(a) operates has yet to be developed. But there is speculation that when too much lipoprotein(a) is present in the arteries, it may compete with plasminogen for access to fibrin in arterial blood clots. Since lipoprotein(a) cannot dissolve fibrin, the dissolution of clots is hampered, increasing the risk of arterial blockage. Another negative function has been suggested as well: Lipoprotein(a), which enters blood vessel walls inside white blood cells known as macrophages, may prompt the release of growth factors by macrophages that thicken artery walls.

Predicting Exercise

Read each question stem, then Stop – Think – Predict. Write down your prediction for each question in a few words.

7. The passage is primarily concerned with

8. Which of the following statements best describes the author's view about research on lipoprotein(a)?

9. According to the passage, which of the following is a difference between lipoprotein(a) and low-density lipoprotein?

10. The author suggests which of the following about the "standard model" (paragraph 1) of the causes of heart disease?

11. According to the passage, research has shown that lipoprotein(a)

12. The passage implies that three-fourths of heart attacks in males under age 60 must occur from

13. Which of the following, if true, would strengthen the theory that lipoprotein(a) contributes to heart disease?

14. As a result of higher levels of blood lipoprotein, factors such as high blood pressure, smoking, and diabetes increase the risk of heart disease.

Matching Exercise

7. The passage is primarily concerned with

   A. discussing the possible role of lipoprotein(a) in some cases of heart disease.
   B. refuting the standard model of risk factors that may lead to heart disease.
   C. examining the evidence for two opposing theories about the function of lipoprotein(a).
   D. proposing that the structure of plasminogen is similar to the structure of apolipoprotein(a).
   E. explaining the cause of heart disease seen in the majority of patients.

8. Which of the following statements best describes the author's view about research on lipoprotein(a)?

   A. Although lipoprotein(a) contributes to heart disease, research on its specific functions has not yet begun.
   B. Research has provided some insight into lipoprotein(a)'s role in heart disease.
   C. Lipoprotein(a) is believed to cause heart disease, but further study of its role has been delayed by technical problems.
   D. Recent test results have determined that lipoprotein(a) does not contribute to heart disease among males under 60.
   E. The research conducted by Richard Lawn is outdated and should not be considered valid.

9. According to the passage, which of the following is a difference between lipoprotein(a) and low-density lipoprotein?

   A. Lipoprotein(a) causes damage to the liver, while low-density lipoprotein causes damage to arteries.
   B. Lipoprotein(a) has only positive functions, while low-density lipoprotein has only negative functions.
   C. Lipoprotein(a)'s functions are taken into account by the standard model of heart disease, while the functions of low-density lipoprotein are not.
   D. Lipoprotein(a) probably contributes to plaque formation by releasing growth factors, while low-density lipoprotein contributes to plaque formation by putting cholesterol into the bloodstream.
   E. Lipoprotein(a) dissolves fibrin to aid in blood clotting, while low-density lipoprotein carries cholesterol to the liver to be used in hormone synthesis.

10. The author suggests which of the following about the "standard model" (paragraph 1) of the causes of heart disease?

    A.   It misidentifies the most frequent causes of heart disease.

    B.   It has been undermined by research on lipoprotein(a).

    C.   It does not account for a significant number of heart disease cases.

    D.   It is no longer credible to most heart disease researchers.

    E.   It also explains the increased number of strokes in heart disease patients.

11. According to the passage, research has shown that lipoprotein(a)

    A.   is more closely related to plasminogen than to low-density lipoprotein.

    B.   functions in the same way as low-density lipoprotein.

    C.   may decrease the risk of heart disease for some people.

    D.   resembles low-density lipoprotein in structure.

    E.   contributes to atherosclerosis by attacking the liver.

12. The passage implies that three-fourths of heart attacks in males under age 60 must occur from

    A.   high lipoprotein(a) levels.

    B.   high levels of low-density lipoprotein.

    C.   high levels of high-density lipoproteins.

    D.   the inability to dissolve fibrin.

    E.   factors other than high lipoprotein(a) levels.

13. Which of the following, if true, would strengthen the theory that lipoprotein(a) contributes to heart disease?

    A. It interferes with clot formation in coronary arteries.

    B. It is more closely related to high-density lipoprotein than to low-density lipoprotein.

    C. It assists in transporting cholesterol to the liver.

    D. It is unable to absorb and transport fatty substances within the body.

    E. It causes the release of growth factors in blood vessels.

14. As a result of higher levels of blood lipoprotein, factors such as high blood pressure, smoking, and diabetes increase the risk of heart disease.

    A. Both the statement and reason are correct and related.

    B. Both the statement and the reason are correct but NOT related.

    C. The statement is correct, but the reason is NOT.

    D. The statement is NOT correct, but the reason is correct.

    E. NEITHER the statement NOR the reason is correct.

STUDY TIP

You can recreate this exercise on your own with any of your Reading Comprehension practice passages. Continue to practice mapping, predicting, and matching to become an expert at the Kaplan Methods.

Running Out of Time Strategy

READ LESS OF THE PASSAGE

→ Read only the first and last paragraphs completely.

→ Read only the first sentence of each body paragraph.

→ Make a shorter map.

→ Skim for proper nouns when tackling questions.

TRIAGE THE QUESTIONS MORE

→ Select an answer for every question.

→ Complete the least time-consuming questions first.

→ Avoid trap answers.

DON'T PANIC

Risk Assessment

(1). Over 40 years ago, former President Nixon signed the National Environmental Policy Act, this nation's first major federal environmental law. **Although** the nation has now witnessed several decades of continuing debate about environmental law, a relatively new element has recently entered the **controversy**: the **use of risk assessment** procedures to determine levels of acceptable risk from threats of hazardous wastes.

(2). Before the development of risk assessment as a decision-making tool, when a spill of a pollutant occurred, a government agency often simply told the responsible party to remove the pollutant. Blah blah blah blah. blah blah, blah blah blah. Blah blah blah blah. blah blah, blah blah blah. Blah blah blah blah. blah blah, blah blah blah. Blah blah blah blah. blah blah, blah blah blah. Blah blah blah blah. blah blah, blah blah blah. Blah blah blah blah. blah blah, blah blah blah. Blah blah blah blah. blah blah, blah blah blah. Blah blah blah blah. blah blah, blah blah blah. Blah blah blah blah. blah blah, blah blah blah. Blah blah blah blah. blah blah, blah blah blah.

(3). But are risk assessments really neutral scientific procedures? Blah blah blah blah. blah blah, blah blah blah.

(4). Environmental decisions based on **current risk assessment procedures** should therefore be viewed primarily as **ethical choices** rather than as technically dictated conclusions. Blah blah blah blah. blah blah, blah blah blah. Blah blah blah blah. blah blah, blah blah blah. Blah blah blah blah. blah blah, blah blah blah. Blah blah blah blah. blah blah, blah blah blah. Blah blah blah blah. blah blah, blah blah blah. Blah blah blah blah. blah blah, blah blah blah. Blah blah blah blah. blah blah, blah blah blah.

15. Which one of the following best expresses the main point of the passage?

    A.   Risk assessment is an improvement over past cleanup methods because it is based more on factual evidence than on intuition.

    B.   Former President Nixon did more than his predecessors to protect the environment from pollutants by approving the use of risk assessment.

    C.   The EPA should mandate the use of thoroughly tested scientific procedures proven to be most effective in removing hazardous waste.

    D.   While the concept of risk assessment is enticing from a scientific viewpoint, this method is so expensive that its use is impractical on a large scale.

    E.   Though risk assessment is perhaps more scientific than previous pollution control measures, the claim that risk assessment is a value-free process is not wholly credible.

16. Each of the following is explicitly mentioned in the passage as part of the risk assessment process EXCEPT one. Which one is the EXCEPTION?

    A.   Visual observation

    B.   Exposure assessment

    C.   Hazard identification

    D.   Risk characterization

    E.   Chemical neutralization

17. The author most likely mentions confidence levels (paragraph 3) in order to

    A.   demonstrate that risk assessment is more scientific than past cleanup methods.

    B.   question the accuracy of post-cleanup visual observations currently in use.

    C.   suggest that the government should eliminate ambiguities in its environmental cleanup agenda.

    D.   show that nonscientific principles can affect the results of scientific processes.

    E.   defend the procedures currently in use for hazard identification and risk characterization.

18. The author suggests which one of the following about pollution cleanup methods that predated the development of risk assessment?

 A. They are considered to be completely ineffective in protecting the environment.

 B. Many environmental professionals are not satisfied with the results produced by these methods.

 C. They are often difficult to apply because they depend on precise scientific measurements.

 D. The best features of these methods should be integrated into the risk assessment process.

 E. They were more effective and less expensive because they did not involve any ethical choices.

19. The passage's reference to the factual and scientific basis of the risk assessment process in paragraph 2 serves which one of the following functions?

 A. It explains the government's unwillingness to choose between older pollution cleanup methods and risk assessment.

 B. It provides background information about how hazardous waste was handled prior to environmental law.

 C. It introduces pollution control policy choices for which there is no a priori assessment method.

 D. It highlights the attitude of environmentalists toward the National Environmental Policy Act.

 E. It underscores the belief of environmentalists that risk assessment is a useful method for controlling pollution.

20. The author of the passage is primarily concerned with

 A. explaining why the government should make explicit the ethical choices involved in environmental cleanup.

 B. highlighting the government's inability to deal effectively with pollution cleanup.

 C. reviewing the evolution of pollution cleanup methods over the past two decades.

 D. proposing a new method for environmental cleanup that incorporates the best features of risk assessment.

 E. suggesting that the government complete additional research on hazardous waste before signing environmental laws.

TAKEAWAY

You can still get points on Test Day even if you don't have time to read every word of the passage. Always use the Kaplan Method to get your easiest points first.

Passage 2

The Corpus Callosum

(1). The evolution of the vertebrate brain occurred primarily in the cerebrum, not the brainstem. The brainstems of all vertebrates, no matter their complexity, are roughly the same size, but this is not so for their cerebrums. The mammal cerebrum has grown so large that it folds in on itself to form a right and left hemisphere, connected by a dense network of neurons called commissures. The most significant of the commissures is the corpus callosum, whose size dwarfs that of the other parts of the mammalian brain.

(2). There is a division of labor in the brain, as in all other parts of the body. There are divisions between the cerebrum and the brainstem, as well as within the various regions of each hemisphere of the cerebrum. However, more interesting for our purposes are the divisions across hemispheres and the role of the corpus callosum, especially in the human brain.

(3). It has long been known that the effects of damage to one hemisphere of the brain often differ radically from the effects of similar damage to the other hemisphere. For instance, injury to the left hemisphere of the human brain often impairs or destroys speech ability, whereas an analogous injury to the right hemisphere does not. For this reason, the left hemisphere has long been regarded as the hemisphere that controls speech and language and that therefore is dominant over its right hemisphere counterpart, which has been characterized as mute, minor, or passive.

(4). However, this reasoning can be misleading in several ways. First, a sizable minority, 10 percent of right-handed people and 35 percent of left-handed people, have their speech areas in the right hemisphere. Second, it has been documented that if the damage to one hemisphere occurs early enough in infant development, the other hemisphere may eventually adapt and take over the tasks usually carried out by its now-damaged counterpart. Indeed, in the mid-nineteenth century, A. L. Wigan, a British physician, performed autopsies on men who apparently led normal lives, yet had only half a brain.

(5). Third, and most importantly, the right hemisphere, though not usually the control center for speech, is far from passive. It controls many visual-motor tasks, so that a person whose right hemisphere is damaged may have difficulty navigating in new areas and fail to recognize familiar surroundings and people. It also seems to be the center for musical talent, so that damage to the right hemisphere may result in a loss of musical ability and yet leave speech unimpaired.

(6). Because of these and other similar facts, people who excel in analytical and verbal tasks, or who are logical and sequential in their problem-solving approaches, are often called left-brained, whereas people who excel at visual and creative tasks, or who are more holistic and novel in the problem-solving are called right-brained. Of course, such characterizations can also be quite misleading.

(7). Of much recent interest is the role played by the corpus callosum, specifically whether—and in what ways—the two hemispheres of the brain can interact when the corpus callosum is severed. In the late 1930s, neurosurgeons discovered that severing the corpus callosum significantly retarded the severity of, or even halted altogether the occurrence of, seizures in certain epileptic patients. More remarkably, these patients seemed to suffer no side effects in personality, behavior, or otherwise. All outward appearances in such patients seemed not to change after their radical treatment. One patient, his sense of humor still intact, even wryly complained of having a "splitting headache."

(8). This naturally led scientists to wonder about the function of the corpus callosum. In the early 1960s, psychobiologist Roger Sperry of the California Institute of Technology began groundbreaking research on just this question. He and his associates designed tests to investigate the behavior of the epileptics who had undergone this radical treatment. In general, the research indicated that in most situations these patients were able to function normally, but placing them under certain carefully controlled conditions led to surprising results. In brief, in certain situations these patients seemed to behave as if they had two separate brains, hence the name "split-brain patient."

(9). Brain wiring is in many cases contralateral, and this holds for the processing of visual information. Thus, information from the right visual field is processed in the left hemisphere of the brain, and likewise information from the left visual field is processed in the right hemisphere of the brain. The same holds true for hand and finger control: The right hemisphere controls the left hand, and the left hemisphere controls the right hand.

(10). Perhaps the most striking of Sperry's discoveries was that visual information could no longer move between the two sides of the brain. In these tests, the subjects were seated in front of a screen on which images could be flashed to either side of her visual field but not the other. The subject's hands were also kept from her own view. This way, the information processed in each hemisphere could be isolated and controlled.

(11). Sperry discovered that if an image was projected to the right visual field of a split-brain patient, thereby being processed in the left hemisphere, the patient could easily describe the image vocally because the left hemisphere controls speech. However, the same image projected only to the opposite, left visual field could not be likewise described; the patient would draw a blank when asked to describe what she saw. Yet in this case, if the patient were asked to point to an object similar to the image seen, she could do so with ease. For instance, in one test, the researchers flashed a dollar sign image to the right visual field of one subject and a question mark to his left visual field. When asked to draw what he saw, he drew the question mark, the image that had been processed in the right hemisphere. When asked to state what he saw, without hesitation he said "a dollar sign," corresponding to the image processed in the left hemisphere. This suggests that the right hemisphere can process the image as well as the left and can even mobilize a non-verbal response, but it cannot provide speech about what it sees in the way that the left hemisphere can.

(12). The same results applied in similar tests for touch, smell, and sound. For instance, when a spoon was placed in the right hand of a test subject, it could be easily identified orally because the left hemisphere controls the right hand; however, the same spoon placed in the subject's left hand could not likewise be identified. One subject even complained about his sinister left hand, which continually tried to undo the work of his right hand, e.g., pulling down his trousers as his right hand attempted to put them on.

(13). These findings initially created quite a stir, sparking a flurry of popular interest in the psychological consequences of these "two realms of consciousness," but most such speculations proved unwarranted by the hard data. Still, the results have had lasting scientific significance, enough to earn Sperry the Nobel Prize in medicine in 1981. They strongly suggest a very sharp and intricate division of labor between the two hemispheres of the brain and also answer, at least partially, the riddle of the corpus callosum: Its function, or at least one of its functions, is to integrate all of the different roles performed by the two hemispheres of the brain.

(14). Of course, the brain is one of the least understood organs of the body, and many questions still remain unanswered. Some researchers are currently investigating the role of the more minor commissures between the hemispheres, and whether these lesser neural pathways can serve to conduct information between the hemispheres even when the corpus callosum is severed. Some scientists also speculate as to the evolutionary reasons behind such lateralization, or specialization between hemispheres. Suffice it to say that Sperry's findings, like all groundbreaking research, both answered many significant questions and raised many new ones.

21. Each of the following kinds of division of labor is specifically mentioned in the passage EXCEPT one. Which one is the EXCEPTION?

    A. That between different types of commissures
    B. That between different areas within the same hemisphere
    C. That between different hemispheres
    D. That between the brainstem and cerebrum
    E. That between different parts of the body in general

22. According to the passage, which of the following actions might result in improvement in a person's seizures?

    A. Removing a portion of the left hemisphere
    B. Removing a portion of the right hemisphere
    C. Severing the corpus callosum
    D. Limiting the visual material presented to the left hemisphere
    E. Providing anticonvulsant drug therapy

23. Which of the following best describes the goal of the passage?

    A. To explain the research conducted by Roger Sperry
    B. To evaluate the effectiveness of split-brain studies
    C. To recommend that split-brain patients receive adequate treatment
    D. To convey details of case studies of split-brain patients
    E. To describe the role of the corpus callosum based on research

24. A brain-damaged patient who is easily disoriented and who fails to recognize family members but whose speech is unimpaired is most likely brain-damaged in which of the following areas?

    A. The right hemisphere
    B. The left hemisphere
    C. Both hemispheres
    D. The corpus callosum
    E. The evidence is inconclusive.

25. A person with left hemisphere brain damage will definitely display which of the following characteristics?

    A.   Slurring of speech and diminished writing ability

    B.   Loss of musical and artistic ability

    C.   Split-brain personality

    D.   None, except under carefully controlled situations

    E.   The age of the patient at the time of the damage determines what effects would be displayed.

26. Which of the following is NOT among the reasons the author cites to support the principle that most changes in the brain leading up to the vertebrate brain occurred in the cerebrum?

    A.   The size of the cerebrum

    B.   The complexity of the cerebrum

    C.   How the cerebrum differs from other parts of the mammalian brain

    D.   The lack of correlation between the size of the brainstem and the complexity of the vertebrate

    E.   The large number of neuronal connections in the corpus callosum

27. Which of the following best describes the author's tone used when describing Sperry's research?

    A.   Laudatory, because Sperry's research explained the evolutionary advantage for lateralization

    B.   Nostalgic about the way that Sperry's findings were able to confirm the results of Wigan's previous research

    C.   Cynical about the ability of the results to help answer the riddle of the corpus callosum

    D.   Intrigued by the possibility that Sperry's findings may help treat epileptic patients without severed corpora callosa

    E.   Earnest about the significance of Sperry's research in determining the function of the corpus callosum

28. The author sometimes speaks loosely of the left and right hemispheres of the brain, but more precisely the hemispheres are of the

    A.   brainstem.

    B.   cerebrum.

    C.   corpus callosum.

    D.   commissures.

    E.   cerebellum.

29. Which of the following most clearly states the riddle of the corpus callosum?

    A.   Severing the corpus callosum seemed to have no ill effect on subjects.

    B.   Severing the corpus callosum leads to split-brain personalities.

    C.   The difference in function between the corpus callosum and the other commissures was unclear.

    D.   Severing the corpus callosum can result in impairment of both right-brain and left-brain functions.

    E.   The corpus callosum's function in humans differs from that in other mammals.

30. The corpus callosum plays an important role in contralateral visual processing. Severing the corpus callosum was shown to decrease the occurrence of seizures.

    A.   Both statements are true.

    B.   Both statements are false.

    C.   The first statement is true, the second is false.

    D.   The first statement is false, the second is true.

31. As a result of Sperry's experiment on the corpus callosum, the right hemisphere was identified as being associated with creative characteristics.

    A.   Both the statement and reason are correct and related.

    B.   Both the statement and the reason are correct but NOT related.

    C.   The statement is correct, but the reason is NOT.

    D.   The statement is NOT correct, but the reason is correct.

    E.   NEITHER the statement NOR the reason is correct.

32. The passage suggests that a more complex vertebrate has a brain with

    A.   a left and right hemisphere.

    B.   a larger brainstem.

    C.   more commissures.

    D.   a larger cerebrum.

    E.   a larger corpus callosum.

33. It can be inferred from the passage that the author believes which of the following regarding the relationship between the left and right hemispheres of the brain?

    A.   The left hemisphere dominates the right.

    B.   The right hemisphere dominates the left.

    C.   Neither hemisphere dominates; each carries out the same functions.

    D.   Neither hemisphere dominates; each carries out different functions.

    E.   The dominating hemisphere is determined by handedness.

34. Which of the following best illustrates the concept of lateralization?

    A.   The right hemisphere of the brain controls the left hand; the left hemisphere controls the right hand.

    B.   Damage to one hemisphere of the brain in young-enough subjects can sometimes be compensated for by the other hemisphere.

    C.   Visual and auditory information is conveyed across the brain hemispheres by the corpus callosum.

    D.   The speech center for a significant number of left-handed people resides in the right hemisphere of their brains.

    E.   The right hemisphere of the brain controls musical ability; the left hemisphere controls speech.

35. Which of the following symptoms is likely to be experienced by a patient with a severed corpus callosum under normal conditions?

    A.   Loss of musical ability

    B.   Debilitating headaches

    C.   Development of a wry sense of humor

    D.   Impaired speech

    E.   Usually no symptoms are present under normal conditions.

36. Which of the following is NOT a piece of evidence from the passage that can be used to explain why it is misleading to consider the left hemisphere as dominant over the right hemisphere?

    A.   The right hemisphere controls visual-motor tasks that are not passive.

    B.   Damage to the right hemisphere may result in a loss of musical talent.

    C.   Early damage to one hemisphere may be compensated for by the undamaged hemisphere.

    D.   A non-negligible percentage of people have their speech areas in the right hemisphere.

    E.   Right-brained people are often characterized as logical and sequential in problem-solving approaches.

Passage 3

Health Benefits of Eye Exams

(1). While eye exams are commonly used to measure and correct vision, they serve an important preventative function as well. There are many different components to a routine eye exam designed to gather information far beyond a patient's visual acuity. Optometrists check each patient's cornea, retina, pupil, iris, optic nerve, ocular pressure, and veins and arteries during an exam. While many of the tests an optometrist completes are intended to provide information about eye health, exams may also reveal important information about overall health, leading to diagnoses of other diseases.

(2). One common component of an eye exam is eye tracking. The patient is asked to look at a target, and his eye movements are recorded while the target moves slightly. This test helps measure eye muscle strength and control, but recent research suggests that eye tracking tests can also serve as an early detection method for Alzheimer's disease. In two studies, the Retinal Amyloid Index and Sapphire II, participants diagnosed with Alzheimer's disease or Parkinson's disease and healthy individuals of various ages were asked to track a light and then look away. It was found that participants with Alzheimer's were up to ten times more likely to make mistakes during these experiments. Healthcare professionals are excited about the possibility that this simple test can help diagnose Alzheimer's because early diagnosis is essential to successful management of the disease.

(3). Pupil dilation is also commonly used as part of an eye exam. When the pupil is dilated, the optometrist can effectively examine the retina and other structures behind the eye. During this part of the exam, special attention is paid to the blood vessels; abnormalities with the vascular system attached to the eye can be a sign of larger cardiovascular problems or diabetes. Sometimes these abnormalities may occur even before other risk factors are apparent.

(4). More specifically, patients may have signs of retinopathy that could be caused by hypertension or diabetes. A patient with retinopathy may have bleeding or oozing, blood vessel narrowing, or damage to the macula or optic nerve. Patients with diabetes are at risk of diabetic retinopathy, which can lead to blindness. In fact, preventive eye care is an important part of the treatment plan for patients diagnosed with diabetes. These patients are at greater risk for glaucoma, cataracts, and other changes in vision.

(5). Interestingly, another disease that can be diagnosed by examining the retina is familial colorectal polyposis. Also known as Gardner syndrome, this autosomal dominant disease is characterized by polyps in the colon. There is no cure for Gardner syndrome, but treatment can help reduce the risk of colon cancer in affected patients. Optometrists may notice specific lesions on the retina that can tip them off to potential problems in the colon. When these lesions are accompanied by scarring without a known reason, such as trauma or other illness, the optometrist will likely inquire about colon health and may send the patient to a gastroenterologist for further examination.

(6). While many of the aforementioned diseases may be diagnosed despite the patient not experiencing other symptoms, sometimes patients will specifically schedule an appointment with an optometrist because they are experiencing eye-related symptoms. These eye-related symptoms may be limited to problems with the eye, oftentimes indicated by changes in vision. For example, blurred, dim, or hazy vision could indicate cataracts, which is a reversible clouding of the vision due to deposits on the lens of the eye. But several symptoms that may point to cataracts could also be indicative of alternate diagnoses.

(7). Many patients affected by cataracts have difficulty with night vision. However, decreased night vision can also be a sign of vitamin A deficiency. Vitamin A can be found in several foods including liver, leafy greens, and carrots. In the eye, vitamin A is used in the form of retinal and combines with the protein opsin to make rhodopsin. Rhodopsin is critical for night and low-light vision. If left untreated, a deficiency of vitamin A can lead to ulcers on the cornea, which can progress to irreversible blindness. Thus, when a patient complains of difficulty seeing in low light, an optometrist will investigate the root of the cause since it could potentially be very serious.

(8). Another symptom that may be concerning to a patient is yellowing of the whites of the eyes, which are known as the sclerae. Yellowing of the eyes is related to jaundice, which also causes yellowing of the skin. The eyes will sometimes yellow before the skin, so this symptom can be an early indicator of an underlying issue. Jaundice is most commonly caused by problems with the liver but can also be a symptom of gall bladder or pancreatic issues. The yellowing is a result of excess bilirubin, which is a product of broken down red blood cells. Increased levels of bilirubin can be a side effect of some medications as well as chemotherapy but can also indicate a serious underlying condition such as bile duct obstruction, liver failure, or pancreatic cancer.

(9). Many other eye-related symptoms can point to still more diseases. Bulging eyes are a symptom of Grave's disease, an autoimmune disease that leads to hyperthyroidism. Chronic drooping eyelids can be caused by the autoimmune disease myasthenia gravis, whereas an acute eyelid droop could potentially be a symptom of a brain aneurysm. The inability to close one eye may be due to Bell's palsy. Sudden changes in vision can also indicate a stroke or a risk of stroke, so medical attention should be sought immediately when these symptoms are experienced.

(10). Healthcare professionals suggest that annual eye exams are important not only for tracking changes in vision but for monitoring overall health as well. At-risk patients such as diabetics should be especially sure to visit their optometrists every year. Healthy adults with no vision problems under the age of 60 may choose to visit an optometrist biannually. Older patients should go to their eye doctors yearly because vision changes more quickly with age. Regardless of patient age, the benefits of regular eye exams are clear.

37. Why are healthcare professionals excited about the results of the Retinal Amyloid Index study?

    A.   Participants with Alzheimer's disease were much more likely to make mistakes in the experiment than other participants.

    B.   Measurements of eye-muscle strength and control can help prevent the development of Alzheimer's disease.

    C.   Previous tests using eye tracking required a target other than light in order to produce meaningful results.

    D.   The test used in the study can be used to diagnose Alzheimer's disease earlier for more effective disease management.

    E.   Eye tracking is already a commonly used test in most routine eye exams performed by optometrists.

38. According to the passage, each of the following is commonly completed as part of an eye exam EXCEPT one. Which one is the EXCEPTION?

    A.   Eye tracking

    B.   Low-light ocular test

    C.   Pupil dilation

    D.   Iris examination

    E.   Visual acuity measurement

39. According to the passage, which of the following is an example of an eye-related disease that patients with diabetes are at greater risk for developing?

    A.   Grave's disease

    B.   Bell's palsy

    C.   Cataracts

    D.   Hypertensive retinopathy

    E.   Jaundice

40. The author discusses the eye-related symptoms of each of the following conditions EXCEPT one. Which one is the EXCEPTION?

    A.   Gardner syndrome

    B.   Myasthenia gravis

    C.   Rhodopsin deficiency

    D.   Drug intoxication

    E.   Retinopathy

41. According to the passage, patients with diabetes are at greater risk for

    A.   limb amputation.

    B.   Alzheimer's disease.

    C.   cataracts.

    D.   cardiovascular problems.

    E.   high levels of bilirubin.

42. Which of the following most accurately depicts the Retinal Amyloid Index as described in the passage?

    A.   The Retinal Amyloid Index was created based on the findings from the Sapphire II experiments.

    B.   Participants who were not previously diagnosed with Alzheimer's were diagnosed with the disease during the study.

    C.   The participants with Alzheimer's and the participants with Parkinson's performed similarly.

    D.   Younger, healthy participants were less likely to make eye tracking mistakes than older, healthy participants.

    E.   Eye tracking as used in the study may help with early detection of Alzheimer's disease in patients.

43. The passage implies that any patient who is having trouble seeing in low light is

    A.   most likely to be experiencing vitamin A deficiency.

    B.   unable to produce rhodopsin because of a deficiency of retinal.

    C.   at greater risk of irreversible blindness if the cause is vitamin A deficiency than if the cause is cataracts.

    D.   likely to develop ulcers on the cornea that will eventually lead to irreversible blindness.

    E.   also likely to experience blurred, dim, or hazy vision due to problems with the lens of the eye.

44. The passage is primarily concerned with

    A.   detailing the components and patient experience of a typical eye exam.

    B.   outlining a recommended schedule for routine visits to an optometrist.

    C.   describing the symptoms of diseases an optometrist might diagnose.

    D.   comparing the diagnostic ability of optometrists and primary care physicians.

    E.   providing additional reasons to visit an optometrist beyond routine visual acuity checks.

45. Which of the following is NOT provided in the passage as a sign of retinopathy?

    A.   Retinal lesions
    B.   Bleeding and oozing
    C.   Damage to the optic nerve
    D.   Blood vessel narrowing
    E.   Damage to the macula

46. When a patient presents with yellowing of the sclerae, the optometrist can be confident that

    A.   the patient has an obstructed bile duct.
    B.   the patient is at greater risk for pancreatic cancer.
    C.   the patient has excess systemic bilirubin.
    D.   the patient's liver is failing.
    E.   the patient is undergoing chemotherapy.

47. Which of the following best aligns with the author's recommendations regarding eye exam frequency?

    A.   A healthy 52-year-old patient visits her optometrist every other year.
    B.   A 33-year-old patient with diabetes visits his optometrist every other year.
    C.   A 47-year-old patient with a family history of Grave's disease visits his optometrist biannually.
    D.   A 67-year-old patient with no known health issues visits her optometrist biannually.
    E.   A healthy 21-year-old patient visits his optometrist every three years.

48. Which of the following, if true, would most strengthen the author's argument about the health benefits of eye exams?

    A.   Optometrists in some states are now legally able to provide immunizations.
    B.   Many health insurance providers do not cover eye care in basic health insurance packages.
    C.   Early treatment of colorectal polyposis reduces the risk of colon cancer by more than 60 percent.
    D.   Vitamin A deficiency has been virtually eradicated in most industrialized nations.
    E.   Periodic acute increases in serum bilirubin occur in 40 percent of people and are usually benign.

49. The sudden onset of eyelid droop may be a symptom of

    A.   hypothyroidism.

    B.   a brain aneurysm.

    C.   myasthenia gravis.

    D.   diabetes.

    E.   macular degeneration.

50. The author briefly discusses the symptoms associated with cataracts in paragraph 6 in order to

    A.   compare the symptoms associated with cataracts with the symptoms associated with vitamin A deficiency.

    B.   provide examples of symptoms that may prompt a patient to schedule an exam with an optometrist.

    C.   recommend that any patient who experiences any of the symptoms seek treatment from an optometrist.

    D.   explain how the optometrist's examination of the lens of the eye can support the diagnosis of cataracts.

    E.   express concerns that serve as a warning about the dangers of letting cataracts go undiagnosed and untreated.

51. According to the passage, how does pupil dilation help an optometrist perform an eye exam?

    A.   Pupil dilation helps the optometrist to measure visual acuity.

    B.   Pupil dilation can be used in place of the eye tracking test.

    C.   Pupil dilation improves the optometrist's ability to view the cornea and iris.

    D.   Pupil dilation allows the optometrist to examine the retina and blood vessels.

    E.   Pupil dilation is only utilized to rule out damage to the vascular system.

52. An optometrist is most likely to refer a patient to a gastroenterologist upon observing

    A.   sudden changes in vision in an otherwise healthy patient.

    B.   yellowing of the sclerae unaccompanied by yellowing of the skin.

    C.   the patient's inability to see in low light.

    D.   drastic changes in vision in a patient with diabetes.

    E.   lesions and scarring on the patient's retina.

Study Plan

After Class: Reading Comprehension 2

Complete Remaining *Lesson Book* Practice Questions	30m	
Practice with Tests and Quizzes		

Practice Tests

Full-Length Test 2	4h 30m	
Full-Length Test 3	4h 30m	
Full-Length Test 4	4h 30m	
Full-Length Test 5	4h 30m	
Full-Length Test 6	4h 30m	
Full-Length Test 7	4h 30m	
Qbank		

STRATEGY 2

TOPICS COVERED

- Strategy Review
- Test Day Preparation
- Test Day Countdown

After this session you will be able to:

- Plan your study calendar appropriately so you know what to do from now until Test Day

Strategy Review

The Kaplan Question Strategy

Step	Purpose	Action
Stop		
Think		
Predict		
Match		

Crisis Prevention

What if I am spending too long on a question?

What if I can't identify what the question is really asking?

What if I can't formulate a prediction?

What if I don't see my prediction in the answer choices?

Kaplan Strategy for Science

STOP

→ Characterize the answer choices.

THINK

→ What is the question really asking?

→ What relevant information do you need?

PREDICT

→ Formulate a framework or prediction for your answer.

MATCH

→ Select the answer that truly meets the requirements of the prediction.

Kaplan Strategy for Reading Comprehension

READ STRATEGICALLY

→ Preview the passage for Topic.

→ Anticipate while reading using Keywords.

→ Map each paragraph's Scope.

→ Determine the author's Tone.

→ Identify the author's overall Purpose.

STOP

→ Characterize the question type.

THINK

→ What is the question really asking?

→ Where is the relevant information you need?

PREDICT

→ Formulate a framework or prediction for your answer.

MATCH

→ Select the answer that truly meets the requirements of the prediction.

Kaplan Strategy for Quantitative Reasoning

STOP

→ Read the question and characterize the answer choices.

THINK

→ What is the question really asking?

→ Choose the best strategy to quickly and accurately solve the problem.

- **Picking Numbers:** Use manageable numbers in place of variables.

- **Backsolving:** Plug the answers into the question stem.

- **Educated Guessing:** Avoid trap answers.

- **Estimating:** Find an answer close to the correct answer.

- **Traditional Math:** Apply classic math formulas.

PREDICT

→ Use the chosen strategy to formulate a framework or prediction for your answer.

MATCH

→ Select the answer that truly meets the requirements of the prediction.

Kaplan Pacing Strategy

Kaplan Triaging Strategy

Kaplan Marking and Review Page Strategy

Pacing Strategies Section by Section

Test Day Preparation

Am I Ready to Take the DAT?

✓ Have I completed all of my Kaplan assignments?

✓ Have I taken enough full-length practice tests to have a sense of my preparedness?

✓ Am I consistently scoring in my desired score range?

✓ Do I have a healthy amount of test anxiety or do I have legitimate areas of concern?

Common Testing Challenges

Symptom	Diagnosis	Prescription
Not finishing sections in time		
Needing to read the same thing over and over		
Narrowing questions down to two answers but picking the wrong choice		
Feeling burned out by Quantitative Reasoning and not performing as well in that section as possible		

Calendar Revision

- Complete any remaining course assignments.

- Recalculate time remaining until Test Day.

- Build in time to take additional full-length tests.

Higher Score Guarantee

- Attend or watch all required sessions. If you are in an instructor-led course, you can use a maximum of two Lessons On Demand as make-up sessions.

- Take all scheduled practice tests.

- Complete the required homework for your course prior to your course expiration date or exam date, whichever is earlier.

Test Day Countdown

The Day Before Test Day

- Plan your day in advance.
- Avoid studying.
- Avoid talking about the DAT.
- Relax.
- Think about your post-test activities.
- Do something you enjoy.
- Eat balanced meals.
- Gather your test materials using the Test Day Checklist.
- Get a good night's sleep.

Test Day Checklist

- ❏ Printout of your confirmation email
- ❏ Personal identification (two)
- ❏ Directions to the test center
- ❏ Extra layers of clothing
- ❏ Snacks and sports drink
- ❏ Tissues
- ❏ Cough drops
- ❏ Painkillers
- ❏ Antacid

The Day of the Test

Before the Test

- Wake up on time.
- Eat your normal breakfast.
- Warm up physically and mentally.
- Wear comfortable clothing and dress in layers.
- Bring all your testing materials.
- Arrive at the test site with time to spare.

During the Test

- Do the tutorial.
- Get comfortable with the computer.
- Triage difficult questions for later.
- Answer every question.
- Reset your mind during the break.
- Focus on what is in front of you.
- Don't discuss the test during the break or after the exam.

After the Test

- Relax and celebrate!
- Tell us about your scores.
- Continue building a strong application.
- Secure letters of recommendation.
- Work on your personal statement.

Test Day Crisis Prevention

What should I do if I...

- start to lose confidence?

- start to lose concentration?

- take too long at the break?

- find the test environment too distracting?

What to Do Now

- Determine whether you are ready to take your test.
- Update your calendar in preparation for Test Day.
- Build your stamina and endurance with testlike practice.
- Contact your teachers if questions still remain.
- Remember that the entire team at Kaplan is here to help you.
- Focus on your successes!

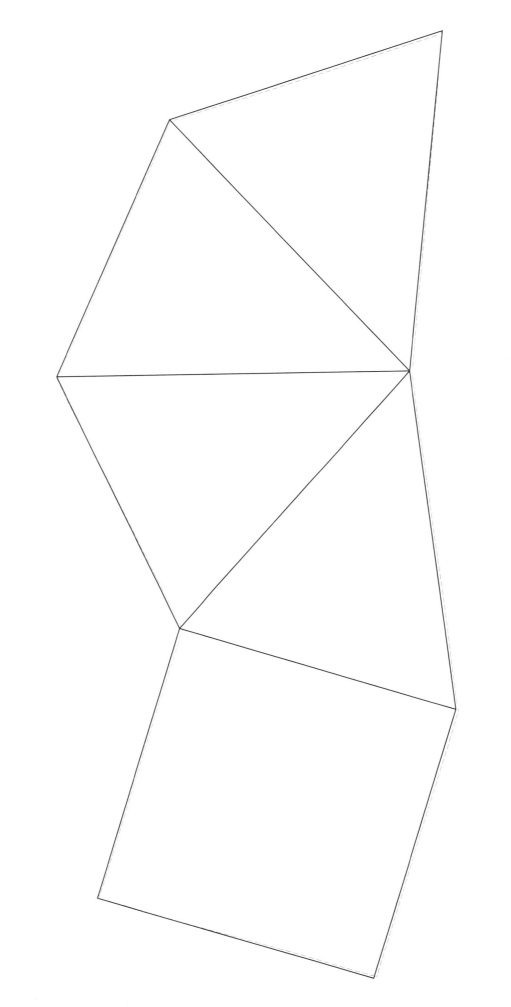

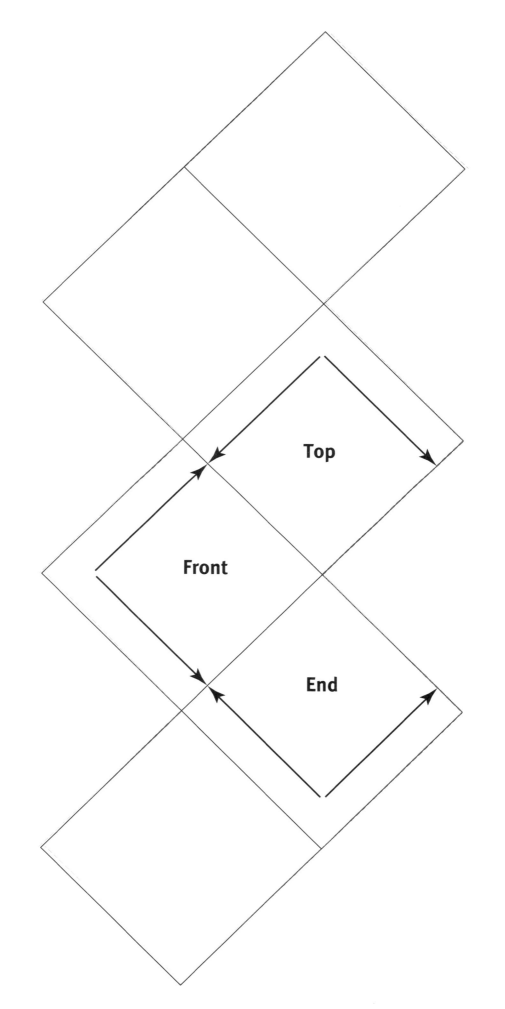

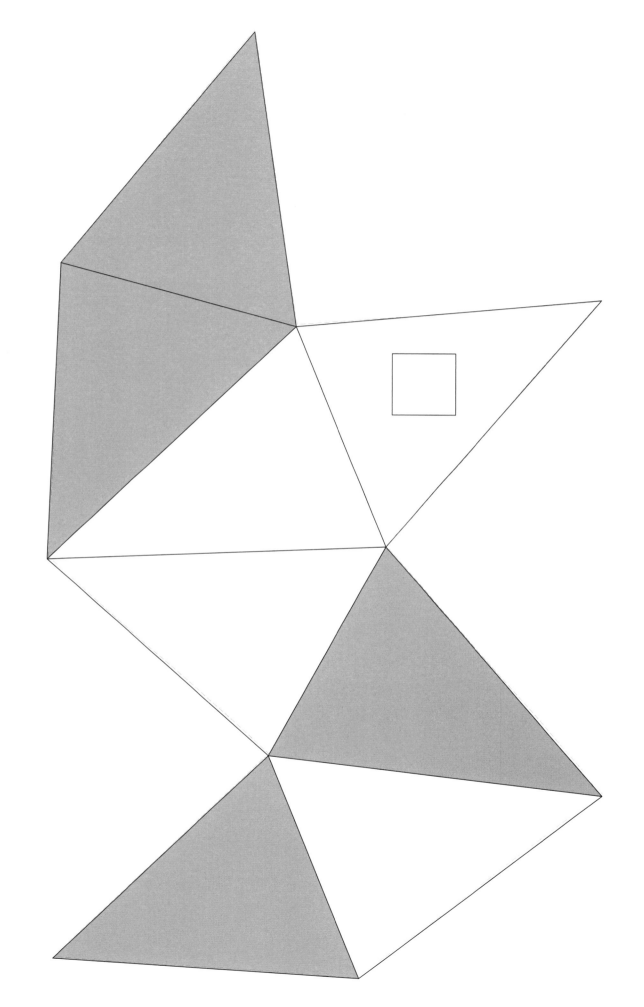